SUPPLY TEACHING

KS2

P4 to 7

AUTHORS
Ann Malpass
Dorothy Tipton

EDITOR
Simon Tomlin

ASSISTANT EDITOR
Dulcie Booth

SERIES DESIGNER
Anna Oliwa

DESIGNER
Anna Oliwa

ILLUSTRATIONS
Ray and Corinne
Burrows

COVER ARTWORK
Andy Parker

Text © 2002 Ann Malpass
& Dorothy Tipton
© 2002 Scholastic Ltd

Designed using Adobe Pagemaker
Published by Scholastic Ltd, Villiers House, Clarendon
Avenue, Leamington Spa, Warwickshire CV32 5PR
Printed by Bell & Bain Ltd, Glasgow

567890   678901

British Library Cataloguing-in-Publication Data
A catalogue record for this book is available from the
British Library.

ISBN 0-439-01977-X

ACKNOWLEDGEMENTS
The Bible Society for Psalm 150 from the
second edition of the *Good News Bible* ©
American Bible Society 1966, 1971, 1976, 1992,
1994 (1994, The Bible Societies/HarperCollins
Publishers Ltd). **Faber and Faber Ltd** for the
use of four lines from 'O what is that sound which
so thrills the ear' from *Collected Poems* by WH
Auden © 1976, WH Auden (1976, Faber and
Faber). **HarperCollins Publishers** for the use
of an extract from *The Magic Pudding* by Norman
Lindsay © Norman Lindsay (HarperCollins
Australia). **Julius Kovac** for the use of an extract
from *Macbeth* by William Shakespeare using the
text from the website www.shakespeare.sk
Learn Library for the use of an extract from
Adventures of Robin Hood by J Walker McSpadden
taken from the website www.learnlibrary.com ©
2000, Learn Library (2000, eBookMall Support).
Penguin Books Limited for the use of four
extracts from *Stig of the Dump* by Clive King ©
1963, Clive King (1963, Penguin).

Every effort has been made to trace copyright
holders and the publishers apologise for any
inadvertent omissions.

Contents

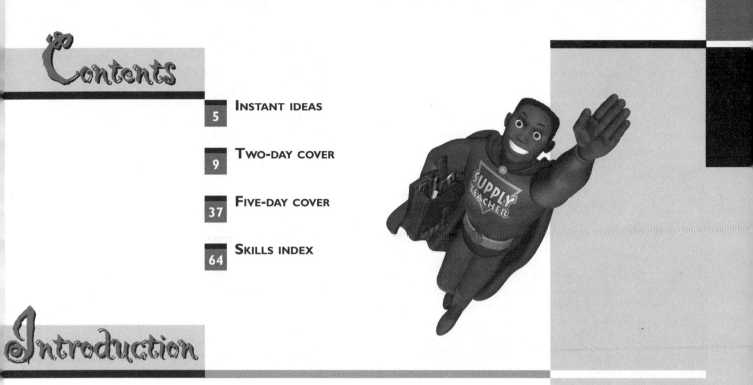

Introduction

Ready to Go: Supply Teaching is intended to be an invaluable resource, offering practical suggestions for teachers who have been called into school at short notice. However, the ideas included can be adapted and modified by all teachers, not just supply teachers, to provide activities for a wide range of cross-curricular themes. The book has been divided into three useful sections for easy reference: Instant ideas, themes for two-day cover and themes for five-day cover.

The 'instant ideas' could be used on many occasions and are a good way to get to know the children quickly. They could also be useful resources for any teacher who is given unplanned and unexpected time with children, when there is not enough time to continue project work.

The second section contains activities for two-day cover on the themes of: Green, Contrasts, Sounds, Time, The wheel and Travel. These are aimed at the supply teacher who has been asked to cover a class in an emergency, where specific programmes of study are not available in time for preparation to be made. The themes are broad based. Each activity within a theme is complete in itself, but has links with all the work undertaken in the two days. The activities cover English and mathematics as a main thrust and all other areas of the curriculum are included.

Section 3 provides activities for five-day cover on the themes of: Living things, Measures, Shakespeare's land and Sunny islands. The activities cover the core subjects of English, mathematics and science, and the foundation subjects of history and geography. All are based on National Curriculum requirements. The themes in this section will either introduce the children to new but appropriate key ideas or reinforce concepts explored by the class teacher but using a different approach.

The themes can be adapted for a shorter time or extended for a longer period by the 'Now or later' section which appears at the end of each theme and each idea can be simplified or made more challenging as required. The photocopiable pages are useful resources to enhance and extend the suggested programmes of study.

PREPARE YOURSELF

This book will give you the opportunity to make appropriate preparations and be ready to go when you receive an unexpected telephone call. It is most important to have prepared a basic kit of items that you are sure to need, but also make use of the school's resources, including the photocopier, to ensure that you have plenty of material ready for the children. A suggested basic kit is:
■ a good story book and/or anthology of poems
■ a modern edition of the Bible and *Religions of the World* by Elizabeth Breuilly and Martin Palmer (Collins)

- digit cards, dominoes, alphabet cards, dice
- a collection of pictures and photographs
- a music tape suitable for listening, dance or discussion
- a whistle, trainers, track suit
- red, black and blue biros, thick black felt-tipped pen
- good eraser, ruler, sharp pencils, pencil sharpener
- Blu-Tack, glue stick, adhesive tape
- scissors
- self-adhesive stickers
- plain A4 paper
- own flip chart or board (for use in preparation)
- your reference number.

Other useful things to take:
- calendar pictures, Christmas and birthday cards
- old photographs and postcards
- suitable magazine pictures
- interesting objects
- collage materials
- dressing-up clothes
- natural materials (fir cones, conkers)
- travel brochures
- found materials (long tubes, egg boxes)
- simple games, particularly those suggested in the text.

What to do when the phone rings
- Take the name and telephone number of the school. Ask for directions.
- Ask for a contact name.
- Establish the age range of the children, brief details of the day's planning and the daily routine.
- Pick up your basic kit.

On arrival
- Find the contact teacher, who should provide you with a daily timetable.
- Take note of fire regulations and security arrangements.
- Enquire about the school's policy on behaviour and discipline and then try to be consistent with what usually happens.
- Establish yourself in the classroom and quickly acquaint yourself with its resources.
- Make yourself ready for the children with a prepared introductory activity.
- Register the children as quickly as possible and move on to the first main activity.
- Establish your routine for the day with the children.
- Adapt the programmes of study in this book to the school's timetable.

THE CHILDREN'S WORK

Each school will have a marking policy and this should be adhered to. Your contact teacher should give you this information. The children's work must be valued at all times and they will of course appreciate positive comments about their work. If the school's policy will allow, it can be rewarding for the children to present their work in individual project books and since most of the photocopiable pages included in this book are of A4 size these could all be clipped together.

Some children may try to take advantage of your position as a supply teacher, so in the longer term assess the standard of their work by looking at previous examples.

RECORDS

It is important that a record of the day's planning is available for the class teacher to see on return. Your assessment of the activities and of significant individual children will be appreciated. Usually there are planning sheets appropriate to each school for you to complete. Informal notes will also be welcome.

Section 1 INSTANT IDEAS

The ideas in this section are for consolidating previous work, introducing new concepts and encouraging quicker responses.

18 INSTANT IDEAS

RESOURCES

You will need copies of photocopiable pages 6, 7 and 8. These will be longer lasting if copied onto card and laminated, cut individually and placed in a box, folder, plastic wallet or stored in a ring binder. They should be kept close at hand for immediate use. A flip chart and a thick, brightly coloured pen will also be needed. The children will need writing materials and paper.

WHAT TO DO

These 18 instant ideas should prove to be an invaluable resource for a teacher, especially one who is meeting a class for the first time. The activities are designed for instant use at times when a teacher has an unexpected moment with the class which needs to be used productively but when there is not time to begin or continue project work. They will also aid a teacher in getting to know a class in a limited time.

The ideas are self-explanatory and easily transferable to a flip chart. Key words or instructions should be copied on to the chart and the children should be given a time limit in which to work the activity. There are many suggestions given for answers but the list is not inexhaustible and the children will doubtless find many more. Make sure that when an 'instant idea' is used there is time for the answers to be heard.

The cards can be used with the whole class, a small group or for individual children, either to re-emphasise a point or when someone has finished a piece of work quickly. They can be an invaluable standby for the busy teacher. They include a variety of ideas. Many of them are not new, but are tried and tested. There are word games, number activities, musical activities, prediction puzzles, starter poems, spelling activities, acrostic poems and many more.

NOW OR LATER

■ Give the children three cards, each with a place, a name and a situation. These could then be used to create a story using them as their main points.

■ Write some random sentences on a flip chart for all to see and invite the children to place them in the correct order so that the writing makes sense.

■ Give the children some unfamiliar words that sound the same but are spelt differently, for example *there/their*, *ware/wear*, *reed/read*, *him/hymn*. They could make a list of these to use in sentences.

■ Give the children some price tags from goods likely to be in a sale and ask them to discount them by 10%.

■ Make a list of electrical goods and ask the children to describe how to use them safely.

■ London cockneys use rhyming slang as part of their everyday speech – ask the children if they know any of the phrases and invite them to create some of their own.

Acrostics

Use the first letter of words linked to a project to write acrostic poems on any subject.

Red
Umbrellas
Let in
Endless
Rain

Millions
Each year
Arrange to
See
Unusual
Railway
Exhibitions

Colours
Are
Personal
And
Can
Indicate
The real
You

Colds
Only
Make
People
Anti
Social
Sniffers

How many...

words from William Shakespeare?

mile	spake	shape	sake
shake	make	will	keepsake
will	rake	am	miss
spear	lake	pill	pier
ear	ream	smile	heap
are	here	spill	hail
spare	mere	pale	swim
lair	leer	pail	raw
hill	pear	speak	mail
ask	reshape	keep	

Try to find more than 40.

Where does it go?

Use the numbers to indicate the place.

heart **1**
lungs **2**
liver **3**
intestine **4**
stomach **5**
skull **6**
kidneys **7**
brain **8**
wrist **9**
ankle **10**

Maths bingo

■ Ask the children to draw a 3 × 3 square and write the answers of the 7 times table (49, 35, 27) into the 9 squares.
■ Call out a number sentence such as 7 x 7. The children cross out the answer.

21	35	28
42	14	56
63	70	49

Develop this idea by combining 7 times and 8 times table answers.

What's the question?

Give the children a number, such as **70**. If this is the answer, what might the question be?

7×10 2×35 $35 + 35$

$40 + 30$ $90 - 20$ $68 + 2$

Try a different number.
If **66** is the answer, what is the question?

$6 \times 11 = 66$ $86 - 20 = 66$

$60 + 6 = 66$ $45 + 15 + 6 = 66$

$2 \times 33 = 66$ $100 - 34 = 66$

Consequences

Everyone needs some paper.
■ Write a boy's name.
■ Fold over name, pass it on.
■ Write a girl's name and fold.
■ Pass it on.
■ Write a place name and fold.
■ Pass it on.
■ Write a time and fold.
■ Pass it on.
■ Write what happens and fold.
■ UNFOLD AND READ.
Jane met Thomas in the library at midnight and they built a fire.

Ready to go! SUPPLY TEACHING

24-hour clock

Hold up the clock. What time is it? Convert the time to a 24-hour clock.

Hold up a digit card. What time is it? Convert the time to analogue time.

Hold up a clock and a 24-hour card. What is the difference in time?

`13.20`

`2.05`

Dictionary time

Make lists of words associated with themes for the children to find in a dictionary. The words should be used in a sentence.

Green	Contrasts
Emeralds	Association
Environment	Negative
Naive	Opposite
Unripe	Silhouette
Jealous	Diverse

Wheel	Time
Rotate	Rhythm
Circumference	Future
Axis	Debate
Angle	Digital
Friction	Clock

Messages

Take the name of a country.
Use the initial letters.
Send a message.

Every **N**ice **G**irl **L**ikes **A** **N**ew **D**ress

Some **P**eople **A**lways **I**nvite **N**ewcomers

I'll **T**ruly **A**lways **L**ove **Y**ou

Are **F**riends **R**eally **I**n **C**hicago **A**merica

Alphabet poems

Create a poem using place names.

Argentina, Austria	K
Brazil and Brum	L
California, Christchurch	M
Durham, here we come	N
E	O
F	P
G	Q
H	R
I	S
J	T **etc**

Continue using the same rhyme

Musical times

Use these notes and rests to make some rhythms.

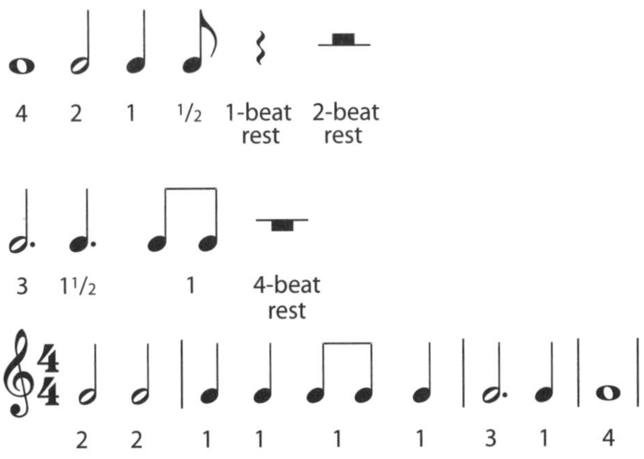

4   2   1   ½   1-beat   2-beat
                      rest   rest

3   1½   1   4-beat
                    rest

4/4   2 2 1 1 1 1 3 1 4

Pyramid poems

Build a pyramid poem using linked words.
Include nouns, adjectives and adverbs.
Here are some starter words.

Animals
Small animals
Small animals run
Small animals run fast
Small animals run fast and silently

Create more on:

People   Rivers

Ready to go! SUPPLY TEACHING

Sign language

Ask the children to create a code for sending secret messages to a friend. It could use letters and/or numbers, for example:

A	B	C	D	E	F	G	H	I	J
25	26	1	2	3	4	5	6	7	8

K	L	M	N	O	P	Q	R	S	T
9	10	11	12	13	14	15	16	17	18

U	V	W	X	Y	Z
19	20	21	22	23	24

Countdown

Give the children a number:

376

Choose 6 numbers at random:

10   5   7   3   8   2

Using +, −, × and ÷, how near to the large number can you get using each number once?

$10 \times 7 = 70$

$70 \times 5 = 350$

$8 \times 3 = 24$

$350 + 24 = 374$

$374 + 2 = 376$

Famous pictures

Look at reproductions of 4 completely different styles of paintings.

Watercolour (Turner)	Oil (Rembrandt)
Modern (Picasso)	Design (William Morris)

Remove the pictures. Describe one of them. Which famous painting is it?

Predictions

What will happen if…

■ you place baking powder inside a balloon, add water and shake?

■ you put a plant in a dark cupboard?

■ you place an egg into a jar of water and add salt or sugar?

■ you place a fizzy drink inside a test tube or bottle with a cork and shake?

■ you attach a balloon to each corner of a handkerchief?

■ you place a piece of string from a low jar of water to a high jar of water?

Try them.

Make it grow

■ Draw one square and colour it red.

■ Surround it and colour these squares green.

■ How many squares are green?

■ Surround the green squares.

■ Colour these squares in blue.

■ How many squares are blue?

■ Continue to enlarge the box, each time predicting how many new squares there are. What is the pattern?

Who came when?

Give the children these names of kings and queens to place in chronological order.

Queen Elizabeth I	Queen Anne
King Alfred	George VI
Queen Elizabeth II	Henry VIII
Queen Victoria	William the Conqueror
Henry VII	Edward VII

This section provides a wide variety of cross-curricular activities for two-day cover on the themes of Green, Contrasts, Sounds, Time, The wheel and Travel.

GREEN

RESOURCES

You will need:

■ paper, writing materials (English)

■ a selection of foreign currencies, copies of photocopiable page 31 for each child and copies of photocopiable page 32 for each pair, board game counters and dice for each pair (mathematics)

■ A3 paper and writing materials for each child, flip chart or board (geography)

■ untuned percussion instruments such as tambours, tambourines and woodblocks (music)

■ a range of different-shaped leaves, paint colour charts, A4 white paper, green/yellow/white paint, brushes and water (art).

WHAT TO DO

English

Introduce the story of Robin Hood, by reading the following extract to the children.

> 'Verily, your lordship,' said Robin, scratching his head, 'I have enjoyed your company so much, that I scarce know how to charge for it.'
>
> 'Lend me you purse, my lord,' said Little John, interposing, 'and I'll give you the reckoning by and by.' The Bishop shuddered. He had collected Sir Richard's debt only that morning, and was even then carrying it home.
>
> 'I have but a few pennies of my own,' he whined; 'and as for the gold in my saddle – 'tis for the church. Ye surely would not levy upon the church, good friends.'
>
> But Little John was already gone to the saddle-bags, and returning he laid the Bishop's cloak upon the ground, and poured out of the portmanteau a matter of four hundred glittering gold pieces. 'Twas the identical money which Robin had lent Sir Richard a short while before!
>
> 'Ah!' said Robin, as though an idea had but just then come to him. 'The church is always willing to aid in charity. And seeing this goodly sum reminds me that I have a friend who is indebted to a churchman for this exact amount. Now we shall charge you nothing on our own account; but suffer us to make use of this in aiding my good friend.'
>
> 'Nay, nay,' began the Bishop with a wry face, 'this is requiting me ill indeed. Was this not the King's meat, after all, that we feasted upon? Furthermore, I am a poor man.'
>
> 'Poor forsooth!' answered Robin in scorn. 'You are the Bishop of Hereford, and does not the whole countryside speak of your oppression? Who does not know of your cruelty to the poor and ignorant – you who should use your great office to aid them, instead of oppress? Have you not been guilty of far greater robbery than this, even though less open? Of myself, and how you have pursued me, I say nothing; nor of your unjust enmity against my father. But on

OBJECTIVES

■ understanding characterisation; creating acrostic poems **(English)**

■ understanding the concept of different currencies; practising addition and subtraction **(mathematics)**

■ understanding and using map symbols and co-ordinates **(geography)**

■ considering environmental issues within a religious framework **(RE)**

■ creating background rhythms **(music)**

■ investigating colour and shape **(art)**

account of those you have despoiled and oppressed, I take this money, and will use it far more worthily than you would. God be my witness in this! There is an end of the matter, unless you will lead us in a song or dance to show that your body had a better spirit than your mind. Come, strike up the harp, Allan!'

'Neither the one nor the other will I do,' snarled the Bishop.

'Faith, then we must help you,' said Little John; and he and Arthur-a-Bland seized the fat struggling churchman and commenced to hop up and down. The Bishop being shorter must perforce accompany them in their gyrations; while the whole company sat and rolled about over the ground, and roared to see my lord of Hereford's queer capers. At last he sank in a heap, fuddled with wine and quite exhausted.

Can the children recall the main characters? There are three of them (Robin, Little John and the Bishop of Hereford). Take Robin Hood as an example. Ask the children to suggest words that could describe him (strong, kind, dependable, agile, thoughtful, considerate). On a sheet of paper, ask the children to write down as many words as they can think of to describe either Robin Hood, Will Scarlet, Friar Tuck, Maid Marion, Little John or the Sheriff of Nottingham if they know the stories of Robin Hood, or one of the characters from the story you have just read if not. The children should work in pairs to complete the activity. Invite them to suggest descriptive words (adjectives or adverbs) to describe their characters. Leave enough time at the end of the session to bring together the children's ideas. Ask them: *Which characters are bad? Which characters are good? Which words tell us that?* Encourage the children to include words other than those in the text.

Show the children what an acrostic is. With the whole class, create a character acrostic. For example:

Robin and his merry men
Over hills and dales they went
Bringing goods from all the rich
In their bags with never a hitch
Never taking from the poor.

Helping those who needed more
Oh they're generous indeed
Oh so generous indeed
Deciding who they need to feed.

In pairs, ask the children to choose a character from the story and write an appropriate acrostic. They can use some of the descriptive words they recorded earlier. Encourage them to read some to each other. The children could mount their poems on the painted leaves they prepare in their art lesson (see Art below).

Mathematics

Show the children the different foreign currencies and talk about holiday spending money. Next ask them to think about the story of Robin Hood and imagine they are shopping in a medieval market. What do they think they would be able to buy there? (Bread, apples, flour, herbs, eggs, oil.) How much might these things cost? Direct the children towards photocopiable page 31, which gives a suggested list of goods at a medieval market and their prices in groats. Ask them to choose four items and then calculate the total cost. Encourage the children to repeat this several times using different combinations of items.

Give pairs of children copies of photocopiable page 32 of the board game 'Going to market'. Tell them they need to work out which would be the shortest route from Sherwood Forest to the medieval market. Is it A, B, C or D? Which is the longest route? Talk about playing board games and ask the children to consider some ideas for rules and procedures. For example, Where do you start? How do you move around the board? Tell the pairs to add some hazards to the routes on the board game. Hazards could include *horse has bolted – move forward three; dropped purse – go back to village.* Encourage them to play the game with dice and counters.

Geography

Can the children remember where Robin Hood lived? (Sherwood Forest.) Give each child a sheet of A3 paper and encourage them to draw an imaginary map of Sherwood Forest. Ask them to think of places they want to include on their maps. You may wish to put a list of places on the flip chart such as market, fingerpost, settlement, lookout tree, castle, church, apothecary, bridge, blacksmith, roads. Ask the children to create symbols of these places for a key and then use these symbols on their map.

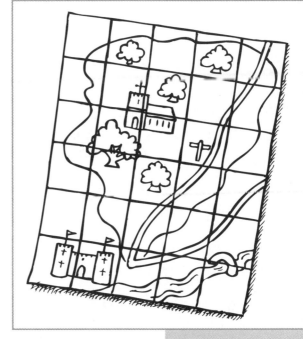

Talk to the children about co-ordinates and make sure that they know how to read them. When they have finished drawing their maps, encourage them to draw a grid with map co-ordinates. In pairs, ask the children to identify places on each other's maps by reading the co-ordinates.

RE

Discuss with the children their ideas on the preservation of living things, in particular plants. Explain that another way we refer to this care today is to say we are talking about a 'green' issue and that there are organised groups around the country which like to meet and discuss this. Why do the children think we should be preserving plant life?

Many of the world religions include a care for nature as part of their beliefs. Christians and Jews are asked to look after the world that God made; Buddhists believe that Buddha 'attained enlightenment' while meditating under a bodhi tree in northern India and this tree is very important to them; Hindus believe that God is present in everything in the world, including plants and animals. Children of different religions should be able to tell the class some of their own beliefs on this subject.

Read to the class the following verse, which is actually a well-known song:

Think of a world without any flowers.
Think of a world without any trees.
Think of a sky without any sunshine.
Think of the air without any breeze.

Ask the children to imagine life in this way. How would they feel? Discuss their answers as a class, and lead them towards a debate on the statement, *There is no need for green plants in the world today.*

Music

Arrange the whole class in a circle. Clap three beats, asking the class to follow your lead. Change the beats to two, four or five, again asking the children to follow.

Read the 'Robin Hood' acrostic to the children (see English above). Clap on *Rob* (1) … *and* (2) … *merr* (3) … *men* (4). Ensure that the children notice that four claps fit the rhythmic pattern. Do they think three will fit? Ask the children to try it, and then to try with five. Help them to recognise that four will be best.

Give the children the untuned percussion instruments (see Resources) to make a four-beat background rhythm. Encourage them to say the acrostic like a rap with a background beat. Some children will enjoy creating a background rhythm to their own acrostic.

Art

Talk about the different colours found in a forest. With the children, look together at the colour charts and encourage them to notice different shades of one colour. Explain that they can experiment to find some shades of green.

Ask them to look at the different shapes and shades of leaves. Can they put them in order from light to dark? On A4 paper, each child should draw a large leaf shape. Ask them to paint the shape using different shades of green to create a leaf effect. (These can be used as a mount for the acrostic poem – see English above.)

NOW OR LATER

■ Children could use the Internet to find out facts about markets in the Middle Ages. (ICT)

■ Herbal medicines were very popular in the Middle Ages. Create an illustrative activity so that the children can identify the difference between dissolving substances such as salt and sugar, and mixing substances such as flour and water. (science)

■ Ask the children to design and make a money bag. Ask them to suggest criteria for making the money bag. *What is the best shape/size/material? What tools and materials are needed?* Get them to plan the procedure. (D&T)

■ Using 'Morning' from *Peer Gynt* (Greig), create a dance sequence to interpret the development of plants in Sherwood Forest, through the seasons, from growth to decay. (PE)

CONTRASTS

OBJECTIVES

■ observing differences in literary characters and characterisation; creating comic strips **(English)**

■ using positive and negative numbers **(mathematics)**

■ becoming familiar with the processes of melting and cooling **(science)**

■ understanding the differences between urban and rural areas **(geography)**

■ empathising with the emotion of jealousy **(RE/PSHE)**

■ contrasting sounds in a musical form **(music)**

■ creating a picture of contrasts **(art)**

RESOURCES

You will need:

■ flip chart or board, writing materials, paper, comic strips (English)

■ number lines, cards showing both positive and negative numbers, photocopiable page 33, flip chart or board, writing materials, paper, a thermometer (mathematics)

■ candles, nightlights, matches, tinfoil dish, small mould (any small container, open dish or jelly mould), food colouring, paper, writing materials (science)

■ an aerial photograph or picture of a contrasting area from the one you are teaching in (rural or urban)(geography)

■ print of *The Return of the Prodigal Son* (by Rembrandt) (RE/PSHE)

■ tuned and untuned instruments (music)

■ cameos or silhouettes, paper, pieces of pressprinting polystyrene (16cm x 10cm), pencils/biros, white printing ink/paint with white glue added, black card (art).

WHAT TO DO

English

Choose a child in the classroom and describe what you see. You may only have seen them briefly but describe external features and try to add something about their character. Ask the children who they think you are describing. Move to a second child and describe in a similar way. *Who is this? How do the children know that you are describing two different people? (For example, contrasting features.) Make a list with the children of the main features of your two people such as *fair/dark, happy/sad, tall/short, glasses/no glasses* and so on. Explain that *contrast* means different and not always opposite.

Read together the following extract from Louisa May Alcott's *Little Women* which describes the main characters in the book.

Margaret, the eldest of the four, was sixteen, and very pretty, being plump and fair, with large eyes, plenty of soft, brown hair, a sweet mouth, and white hands, of which she was rather vain. Fifteen-year-old Jo was very tall, thin, and brown, and reminded one of a colt; for she never seemed to know what to do with her long limbs, which were very much in her way. She had a decided mouth, a comical nose, and sharp, grey eyes, which appeared to see everything, and were by turns fierce, funny or thoughtful. Her long, thick hair was her one beauty; but it was usually bundled in a net, to be out of her way. Round shoulders had Jo, big hands and feet, a fly-away look to her clothes, and the uncomfortable appearance of a girl who was rapidly shooting up into a woman, and didn't like it. Elizabeth – or Beth, as everyone called her – was a rosy, smooth-haired, bright-eyed girl of thirteen, with a shy manner, a timid voice and a peaceful expression, which was seldom disturbed. Amy, though the youngest, was the most important person, in her own opinion at least. A regular snow maiden, with blue eyes and yellow hair, curling on her shoulders, pale and slender and always carrying herself like a young lady mindful of her manners. What the characters of the four sisters were we will leave to be found out.

Ask the class to make their own list of characteristics for each person (Margaret – *plump*, *fair*, *pretty*; Jo – *tall*, *thin*, *brown*, *untidy*). The children could then use these lists to find pairs of contrasting words (*plump/thin*, *grey eyes/bright eyes*, *sweet mouth/firm mouth*). Encourage them to share their ideas together.

Give each child a comic strip to look at for a short time. Divide the class into pairs and encourage the children to discuss the contrasting characteristics that make up successful comic-strip characters (*fat man/thin man*, *old/young*, *good-natured/bad-natured*, *strong/weak*). Invite some discussion about these. Create a situation with all of the children to include two contrasting characters, a dog, a frozen pond, a ladder and a piece of rope. In pairs, ask the children to write and draw a comic strip to show their own interpretation of the situation using speech bubbles and a brief explanatory text. Make a class display of the results.

Mathematics

Introduce the children to positive and negative numbers as contrasting numbers by drawing a number line and placing 0 in the middle. Ask the children which numbers they think come after the 0 and which before. Give everyone a strip of paper to draw their own number line showing positive and negative numbers. Using the pre-made cards showing both positive and negative numbers, ask a child to take one at random and place it in a position where everyone can see it. The next person must place their random number in place in relation to the first one. Continue until all the numbers have been correctly placed. Repeat until everyone has placed a number. Can anyone think of anywhere that they have seen positive and negative numbers used? (For example, thermometer, flood line, sea level, golf scores.)

Discuss together the way you could tell if a river had recently been in flood or if there had been a drought. (You would be able to see the silt and debris in the surrounding vegetation when in flood or a lack of vegetation on the river banks when in drought.) Where would the children go to look? Ask them to imagine they are by the River Severn (or your local river) and by a bridge there is a marker showing the river levels for various years. These might be the ones shown on photocopiable page 33. After discussing the levels the children should work through the questions on the photocopiable sheet.

Draw a number line, with some positive and negative numbers missing, for everyone to see and ask the children to complete it. Make sure everyone has a final correct answer. Show the whole class a thermometer and ask them to look at it closely to see the positive and negative numbers. Discuss when the mercury would be on the positive mark and when it would be on the negative.

Show the children two of the positive or negative number cards and ask what the difference is. For example, –2 to +3 is a difference of 5; or –7 to +4 is a difference of 11. Give the children a list of positive and negative temperatures in two columns, and ask them to work out the difference between the two.

Science

You will need to be sure that the science lesson is in the afternoon so that you and the children can light a nightlight candle during lunchtime, leaving it in a safe place to burn so that the wax can be used in the lesson.

Tell the class that they are going to learn about the contrasting states of substances. Show them a solid candle and let them touch, smell and feel it, discussing the observable qualities. Refer them to the solid candles that were previously lit and look together at how they have melted. Notice the differences in their appearance. Ask everyone to make a list of other household substances that will melt in heat and which, when cooled, will solidify (such as butter, margarine, chocolate, boiled sweets). Can the children describe the process? Have some of these additional items for the children to see, and illustrate them melting over boiling water using a tinfoil dish and then cooling over cold water and solidifying.

Collect the melted wax from the small candles and place it all in one mould (see Resources for ideas) and add some colouring while it is still warm. Cool it quickly by using cold water and watch the change. Remove it from the mould before it is completely solid and notice the change of state. Ask the children to record the change from solid to liquid in a series of labelled diagrams.

Geography

Ask the children to imagine that they are going on a hot-air balloon ride or a helicopter ride over the area where the school is located. What would they expect to see? (For example, clusters of houses, fields, river, streets, tops of buildings.) Show them the aerial photograph or picture of the area that is in contrast to their own and ask them to identify the differences.

Together, make a list of the main features of the children's own area – for example, fields, farms, footpaths, churches, isolated shops, a pub, tractors, cattle, sheep and so on. Ask the children to copy this list and to write another list of the things they would expect to see if they were travelling over the contrasting area. Give everyone a piece of paper which they must divide in half, drawing their bird's eye view of their own area in one half, with the contrasting area drawn in the other half. The drawings do not need to be accurate but everything on the lists you made earlier should be represented.

RE/PSHE

If it is possible show the children a print of the Rembrandt painting *The Return of the Prodigal Son* (it is in the Hermitage Museum in St Petersburg). This painting shows a forgiving father with his hand on the shoulder of a returning son and the jealous older brother looking on. The attitudes of the two people contrast with each other and this can be seen in the painting. Read the following story of the prodigal son from *The Message* by Eugene Peterson or from any modern Bible.

The story of the lost son

There once was a man who had two sons. The younger said to his father, 'Father, I want right now what's coming to me.'

So the father divided the property between them. It wasn't long before the younger son packed his bags and left for a distant country. There, undisciplined, he wasted everything he had. After he had gone through all his money, there was a bad famine all through that country and he began to hurt. He signed on with a citizen there who assigned him to his fields to slop the pigs. He was so hungry he would have eaten the corncobs in the pig slop, but no one would give him any.

That brought him to his senses. He said, 'All those farmhands working for my father sit down to three meals a day, and here I am starving to death. I'm going back to my father. I'll say to him, "Father, I've sinned against God, I've sinned before you; I don't deserve to be called your son. Take me on as a hired hand." ' He got right up and went home to his father.

When he was still a long way off, his father saw him. His heart pounding, he ran out, embraced him, and kissed him. The son started his speech: 'Father, I've sinned against God, I've sinned before you; I don't deserve to be called your son ever again.'

But the father wasn't listening. He was calling to the servants, 'Quick. Bring a clean set of clothes and dress him. Put the family ring on his finger and sandals on his feet. Then get a grain-fed heifer and roast it. We're going to feast! We're going to have a wonderful time! My son is here – given up for the dead and now alive! Given up for lost and now found!' And they began to have a wonderful time.

All this time his older son was out in the field. When the day's work was done he came in. As he approached the house, he heard the music and dancing. Calling over one of the houseboys, he asked what was going on. He told him, 'Your brother came home. Your father has ordered a feast – barbecued beef! – because he has him home safe and sound.'

The older brother stalked off in an angry sulk and refused to join in. His father came out and tried to talk to him, but he wouldn't listen. The son said, 'Look how many years I've stayed here serving you, never giving one moment of grief, but have you ever thrown a party for me and my friends? Then this son of yours who has thrown away your money shows up and you go all out with a feast!'

His father said, 'Son, you don't understand. You're with me all the time, and everything that is mine is yours – but this is a wonderful time, and we had to celebrate. This brother of yours was dead, and he's alive! He was lost and he's found!'

Ask the children how they think they would have felt if they had been the elder brother. Jealous? Angry? Happy? Relieved? Most children will feel angry and jealous but the father is just the opposite. He is happy and forgiving. His mood contrasts with that of his older child. Ask the children to discuss when they feel jealous and lead on to discussions about what they can do about it.

Music

Tell the children that they are going to create a 'contrast rondo' and that a rondo in music simply means one tune followed by another, but the first tune keeps coming back. It is easiest to explain if you write the letters *A B A C A D A* where the children can see them and explain that *A* is the tune that recurs. Ask which sounds in music they think might be contrasts (wood and metal, high and low, bright and dull). Decide which sounds you would like for each letter (for example, *A* – wood; *B* – metal; *C* – strings; *D* – skin) and divide the class into four groups. Give each group a letter (A, B, C or D) and everyone an appropriate instrument and then invite them to make a short piece of music using only the instruments made of their material. The tune can be as simple as one child playing a marching rhythm, with a second joining in, then a third, until the whole group is playing with each sound gradually falling away leaving the first sound on its own. Alternatively, each group could play softly and gradually get louder and then softer again. Once the groups have created their pieces, listen to each one and then place together as a contrasting rondo, pointing to group A to play between each section. Explain to the children that many famous composers (Bach, Mozart, Beethoven) used the rondo form in their music. Encourage the children to perform and record the whole piece for everyone to listen to.

Art

Talk to the children briefly about cameos and silhouettes, both of which show good use of contrasts. Some children will have seen one before (family members may have cameo brooches at home) and will be able to describe it. Wherever possible, have an example of one of these to show the children.

In pairs, ask the children to look carefully at the side view of their partner's head and shoulders, and make a pencil sketch of it. Give each child a piece of the pressprinting polystyrene and ask them to redraw their image on it with a sharp pencil or biro (they should not draw too close to the edge of the polystyrene). They should then paint over this with printing ink or paint mixed with white glue and print the image onto black card.

NOW OR LATER

■ Contrast the lifestyle of the rich and the poor in Victorian England. Give the children sentences to finish, such as *I am a kitchen maid and I live in a large and very grand house in the centre of London…* or *I am a railway worker and my life is very different from that of my master…* (English)

■ Have two dice available of different colours. One colour represents positive numbers and the other negative numbers. Ask the children to subtract one from the other. (mathematics)

■ Look at the difference between condensation and evaporation through an exploration of the water cycle. (science)

■ Children could make a collage out of contrasting materials (rough and smooth, light and dark). (art)

SOUND

OBJECTIVES

■ understanding how a writer creates atmosphere; using similes in poetry **(English)**

■ understanding, estimating and measuring capacity **(mathematics)**

■ observing how vibrations create sound **(science)**

■ discovering how sound is used in praise **(RE)**

■ understanding the use of Italian musical terms in traditional notation **(music)**

■ responding to the musical sounds used by a composer to create a dance **(PE)**

RESOURCES

You will need:

■ flip chart or board, writing materials (English)

■ containers of different sizes, water, measuring jug, photocopiable page 34 (mathematics)

■ a selection of instruments to show vibrations, including a violin or guitar, drum and piano (science)

■ a selection of tuned instruments (woodwind – recorder, saxophone, clarinet, flute; string – violin, viola, cello, double bass; brass – trumpet, horn, cornet, euphonium; percussion – any instrument from the percussion trolley such as xylophone, glockenspiel, chime bars and metallophones as well as any orchestral instruments) and untuned instruments (triangle, drum, castanets, guiro, casaba) (music)

■ a recording of *Danse Macabre* by Saint-Saëns (PE).

WHAT TO DO
English

Introduce this activity with a few moments of silence and ask the children to tell you what they can hear. You could create other situations and ask them to imagine background sounds. For example, *You are sitting at a bus stop – what might you hear?* or *You are lying on a sandy beach in the sunshine on a hot July day – which sounds do you hear?* Explain that there are very few times when one cannot hear anything at all (except in a sound-proofed room) and descriptions of sounds are important to writers in creating convincing scenes.

Read to the children the following excerpt from *The Railway Children* by E Nesbit.

That was a very odd noise indeed – a soft noise, but quite plainly to be heard through the sound of the wind in the branches, and the hum and whir of the telegraph wires. It was a sort of rustling, whispering sound. As they listened it stopped and then it began again.

And this time it did not stop, but it grew louder and more rustling and rumbling.

'Look' – cried Peter, suddenly – 'the tree over there!'

The tree he pointed at was one of those that have rough grey leaves and white flowers … And as Peter pointed, the tree was moving – not just the way trees ought to move when the wind blows through them, but all in one piece, as though it were a live creature and were walking down the side of the cutting.

'It's moving!' cried Bobbie. 'Oh look! And so are the others. It's like the woods in *Macbeth*.'

'It's magic,' said Phyllis, breathlessly. 'I always knew the railway was enchanted.'

It really did seem a little like magic. For all the trees for about twenty yards of the opposite bank seemed to be slowly walking down towards the railway line, the tree with the grey leaves bringing up the rear like some old shepherd driving a flock of green sheep.

…The trees moved on and on. Some stones and loose earth fell down and rattled on the railway metals far below.

'It's *all* coming down,' Peter tried to say, but he found there was hardly any voice to say it with. And, indeed, just as he spoke, the great rock, on the top of which the walking trees were, leaned slowly forward. The trees, ceasing to walk, stood still and shivered. Leaning with the rock, they seemed to hesitate a moment, and then the rock and trees and grass and bushes, with a rushing sound, slipped right away from the face of the cutting and fell on the line with a blundering crash that could have been heard half a mile off. A cloud of dust rose up.

'Oh,' said Peter, in awestruck tones, 'isn't it exactly like when coals come in? … The 11.29 hasn't gone by yet. We must let them know at the station, or there'll be a most frightful accident.'

'Let's run,' said Bobbie, and began.

A fuller version of this can be found in *The Puffin Book of Classic Children's Stories*. There are many references to sounds in this passage. Ask the children to tell you which ones they can remember most clearly (the wind in the branches, the humming and whiring of the telegraph wires, the stones rattling on the railway metal). Once you have talked about these descriptions, read the passage again.

Ask the children to imagine that they are sitting on a railway embankment, waiting to see the trains, and they hear an unusual sound. What might it be? Ask the children for their ideas, and encourage them to write them down. *Does the sound come from the tunnel, the banks or on the rails? What is it?* Explain that a good way to describe things is to say they look or sound like something else (a simile). For example, *The train sounded like a lion roaring as it rushed out of the tunnel.* Write down the children's 'unusual sound' suggestions and ask each child to write their own sound similes for them. Listen to some of them read by the children.

Read together the following verse from the WH Auden poem 'O what is that sound which so thrills the ear':

> O what is that sound which so thrills the ear
> Down in the valley, drumming, drumming?
> Only the scarlet soldiers, dear,
> The soldiers are coming.

Use the structure, pattern and descriptive nature of this verse as a model for the children to write their own poem about the railway bank and its sounds. For example:

> What is this sound as transfixed I stand?
> Tiny stones rattle and slip down the bank
> Trees in their majesty walk hand in hand
> They're marching, they're marching in military rank.

Make sure the children understand that, while rhyming is useful, it is not essential in this kind of poetry where descriptions are so important. Read the poems, then discuss which is considered to be the most effective and why.

Mathematics

Before the lesson begins, set up seven containers of water so that all the children have a clear view of them. They can be different sizes and should have a random amount of water inside (glass will give the clearest sounds). Tap each one for the children to listen to. What do they hear? What do they notice? (They should hear that the one with the largest amount of water has the lowest sound.) Can the children estimate how much water is in each of the containers? Complete a chart together as in Figure 1. Measure with the children the actual amount in each container and add those results to the chart. How close were their estimates?

Container	Estimate	Measure
	500 ml	650 ml

Figure 1

Divide the class into groups of four. Each group will need some containers of different shapes and sizes. Without using liquids, ask the children to estimate and write down how much liquid they think would be needed to fill the container. Make sure that the children understand that they are measuring in litres and millilitres. Once estimated, the containers should be arranged in order of size. Make time for a discussion as to why a tall thin container might hold more or less liquid than a short fat container. Give each group the opportunity to fill their containers, measure the liquid and record their results. Discuss together any interesting findings.

Direct the children to photocopiable page 34. They must draw a line where they think the amount shown would be, (remind them to view the bottle from eye level rather than looking down into the container.) Afterwards, they must estimate where the water line is in the jars shown in the second column and write down the amount. Once this is complete the children should work in pairs and will need the measuring jug, water and an unmarked container (plastic bottle). One child should measure some water into the measuring jug without their partner seeing the accurate measurement, then pours it into the unmarked container. The other child then estimates what is there and writes it down, then pours it back into the measuring jug. Is the amount correct? The children can repeat the activity several times.

To bring the activities to a close, encourage the children, as a whole class, to create a descending sounding scale from the containers of water.

Science

Bring the selection of instruments into the classroom and ask the whole class to listen to each instrument, preferably being played by a child who is having lessons on it, and discuss how the sound is made. Make sure that you emphasise that sounds are created when an object vibrates and that by blowing, plucking, shaking or banging an instrument, a vibration is created in the air. Demonstrate this by plucking a violin or guitar string and watching the string move. Tell the children that sound travels very fast through the air in waves and explain that the quality of the sound will vary according to the size or the shape of the instrument. Use a drum to demonstrate further. Show them that by hitting the skin, vibrations are set up in the air. Explain that these are called sound waves, but we cannot see them. They travel from the instrument to the ear of the listener. If possible, take the front off the piano and show the children how the hammers hit the strings, causing them to vibrate. Then press down the right pedal and watch the dampers move away from the strings to allow the strings to vibrate even longer. Ask the children to look at, try and experiment with a selection of instruments in a short, agreed time, to see for themselves how the instruments vibrate.

RE

Read together this version of Psalm 150 below, and discuss with the children what a psalm is.

Praise the Lord!
Praise God in his Temple!
Praise his strength in heaven!
Praise him for the mighty things he has done.
Praise his supreme greatness.

Praise him with trumpets.
Praise him with harps and lyres.
Praise him with drums and dancing.
Praise him with harps and flutes.
Praise him with cymbals.
Praise him with loud cymbals.
Praise the Lord, all living creatures!
Praise the Lord!

Explain that a psalm is like a song or a poem of praise which is sung and that many psalms mention the sounds of the instruments of the time when they were written. Do the children know what a lyre, harp, trumpet, flute or cymbal look like? What do the class think would be the equivalent of a psalm today? (For example, a pop song, rap, poem.) Collect together a list of things that the children would like to give thanks for (for example, good food, natural world, gardens) and write a 'Thank you rap'. It could be in the following style:

I was walking in the city the other day
And I felt good, so what could I say
I said 'Thank you for the things I like to eat
I like burgers and chips, sausages and meat.
I'm glad I've got some shoes to wear
Though I'll be happy when I've got another pair.
My jeans are warm, and that's a good thing
I feel so happy, I want to sing
THANK YOU.'

Choose a child who has a strong sense of rhythm and ask them to beat out a strong background beat for the rap while the class chants it.

Music

Re-read the E Nesbit description of the railway bank to remind the children of the sounds suggested. Explain to them that they are going to create a sound picture of this incident using musical instruments for the sounds, and that they will be responding to the Italian instructions that musicians all over the world use. The sound picture will be in response to the Italian words. Have a look at these words together and discuss their meanings:

Peace/calm (calmato), rustling (crescendo/diminuendo, getting louder and softer), whispering (piano/softly), walking (marcato), rattling (staccato), falling earth (glissando), stop (fermata), shivering (vibrato), rushing (presto), crash (fortissimo).

Write the Italian words where everyone can see them and divide the class into small groups. Each child in the group should choose from the selection of tuned and untuned instruments and should try to create all the appropriate sounds (calm, getting louder and so on). Each of the groups should choose a leader to conduct the beginning and end of their sound. Limit the time for this as it will be noisy, but experimentation should be encouraged. Hear one or two groups, leaving time to create the whole picture together. To do this, point to the word, all the children should play the sounds and gently move to the next word and sounds, without anyone speaking. With practice, this can produce a most effective sound picture and the children will have learned a few Italian musical terms.

PE

This session of dance will be based on the story told in music by the French composer Saint-Saëns called *Danse Macabre*. Death is the main character and he dances on and around the ancient Etruscan tombs. Explain to the children that Death plays a violin as he dances and the skeletons come from the tombs to join in the macabre dance. Explain that *macabre* means frightening or spooky.

Listen together to the music, and choose three sections for the children to dance to. The first will be at the beginning when Death tunes up his violin and dances. The second section will include a dance by the skeletons and the third will be near the

end of the music when you can clearly hear the cockerel crow and the skeletons return to their graves. Ask one child to be Death and the others to be the skeletons. At the end of the session give time for the children to describe how they felt when dancing to this music and ask if they thought the composer used the instrumental sounds well to describe the story.

NOW OR LATER

■ Find poems that use alliteration, such as the traditional rhyme 'One misty, moisty, morning', and show the children how effective these sounds can be (explosive sounds – *bim, bam, boom*; or sleepy sounds – *swaying softly, sleeping soundly*) in writing poetry. (English)

■ Ask the children in pairs to make a telephone by using two plastic cups and a piece of string. One person speaks and one person listens. The voice makes the air inside the cup vibrate; this vibration makes the string vibrate. Sound waves travels along the string and causes the second cup to vibrate. The sound waves strike the ear of the listener and he or she hears what is being said. (science)

■ Find information about Alexander Graham Bell and the invention of the telephone to discuss with the children. (history)

■ Encourage the children to look at a calendar picture and imagine what the sounds would be like if the picture came to life. In small groups, encourage the children to create their own representation of those sounds. (music)

TIME

RESOURCES

You will need:
■ paper, writing materials (English)
■ large 24-hour time cards, a set of cards with times written in words, photocopiable page 35 made into an OHT, an OHP, paper, writing materials (mathematics)
■ an anglepoise lamp, enough torches for one between each pair of children (science)
■ a feely bag or box containing a range of artefacts from Victorian times to the present day (such as a modern vase, a woodwork tool, a flat iron, bellows, a carpet beater, a mincer, horse brass, a bobbin, a button hook, a shoemaker's last, a CD, vinyl record, a modern and an old bottle, a plastic flowerpot, a ration book and so on), paper, writing materials (history)
■ music to accompany a march, waltz and lullaby; tuned and untuned musical instruments (music)
■ paper, writing materials (D&T).

OBJECTIVES

■ writing from their own imagination and interpreting a situation through drama (**English**)
■ recognising 24-hour times and using a timetable (**mathematics**)
■ understanding why shadows are formed (**science**)
■ developing historical enquiry (**history**)
■ recognising differences in time (**music**)
■ designing a timepiece, identifying materials and planning its assembly (**D&T**)

WHAT TO DO

English

Give each child a piece of paper. Tell the children to close their eyes and say: *A machine has just landed in the centre of the room, the door is open, a voice is saying, 'Travel with us to a different time zone'.* Ask the children to step inside and imagine that they are going there with a friend. Tell them they need to decide which time zone they would like to go to and to write this on a piece of paper together with why they are going there. Listen to some of the children's ideas. Now invite the children to write a plan of what is going to happen to them. Ask them: *Is it past, present or future time? Who will be there?* Ask them to create a problem they will encounter in their chosen time zone and how they are going to solve it. Share some of the children's ideas and if there is time, ask them to write the story individually.

Read the following extracts from *Stig of the Dump* by Clive King.

> Barney lay quiet and looked around the cave again. Now that his eyes were used to it he could see further into the dark part of the cave.
>   There was somebody there!
>   Or Something!
>   *   *   *
>   Something or Somebody, had a lot of shaggy black hair and two bright black eyes that were looking very hard at Barney.
>   'Hullo!' said Barney.
>   Something said nothing.
>   'I fell down the cliff,' said Barney.
>   Somebody grunted.
>   'My name's Barney.'
>   Somebody-Something made a noise that sounded like 'Stig'.
>   'D'you think you could help me undo my feet, Mr Stig?' asked Barney politely. 'I've got a pocket-knife'...
>   *   *   *
>   The Thing sitting in the corner seemed to be interested. It got up and moved towards Barney into the light. Barney was glad to see it was Somebody after all. 'Funny way to dress though,' he thought, 'rabbit skins round the middle and no shoes or socks.'
>   *   *   *

> Barney got up and went into the dark part of the cave.
>
> He'd never seen anything like the collection of bits and pieces, odds and ends, bric-à-brac and old brock, that this Stig creature had lying about his den. There were stones and bones, fossils and bottles, skins and tins, stacks of sticks and hanks of string. There were motor-car tyres and hats from old scarecrows, nuts and bolts and bobbles from brass bedsteads. There was a coal scuttle full of dead electric light bulbs and a basin with rusty screws and nails in it. There was a pile of bracken and newspapers that looked as if it were used for a bed. The place looked as if it had never been given a tidy-up.
>
> 'I wish I lived here,' said Barney.

Stig was a caveman who was living in a rubbish tip. He had only caveman ideas, no language, no clocks and no time. He was inventing things from the rubbish that he found. Ask the children how they know that Stig came from a different time (his clothes, the things he's collected, what he's making, his lack of language). In pairs, encourage them to dramatise the scene where Barney meets Stig. Invite them to write a drama script for this part of the story.

Mathematics

Ask the children where in their home they have a 24-hour clock (microwave, video, watch, oven). *What is a 24-hour clock? Did your great-grandparents have one?* What did they have? (They would have had a 12-hour clock.) Hold up the large 24-hour cards, with different times written on them, for the children to identify the time of day. For example, 14.25 is the same as 2.25pm and 25 minutes past 2. Select cards randomly and arrange them so that everyone can see them. Work with the class to arrange the cards from earliest to latest.

Have the other set of time cards, with the times written in words (for example, *twenty minutes to ten, ten minutes to seven* and so on). Ensure that these times correlate exactly with the first set of cards prepared. Ask the children to match the two sets of cards.

Using the first set of cards, give the children a further opportunity to practise recognising the times. Hold up two cards with different times – one a 24-hour clock time, the other a 12-hour clock time. Ask the children if they began a journey at the first time and arrived at the second time, how long the journey would have taken.

Make an OHT to show the timetable on photocopiable page 35. Ask questions associated with information on the timetable. For example: *When do I need to be at the station to catch the first train to Edinburgh/York/Derby/Chester? Which train leaves first? How long does it take to get to Chester if I catch the train at 12.38?* Ask the children to calculate how long it takes for each train to reach its destination.

Ask the children to plan a journey lasting 35 minutes, with the train stopping at three stations. *What time does the train arrive at each of the stations? What time does it arrive at the final destination?* Encourage the children to choose their own time to begin the journey. Make sure that the train times add up to 35 minutes.

Science

This lesson focuses on shadows. The children need to understand that the shadows appear when light is blocked from the Sun, that shadows change every day and that they change in length. Introduce them to the concept that shadows are formed when an object blocks the light from the Sun. If it is a sunny day there will be no problems in seeing shadows, otherwise you need to create them by using a light source (such as a torch or lamp) and objects to block the light.

Take the children and an anglepoise lamp to a darkened room or darken the classroom. Tell the children to make shadows on a wall with their hands and discuss how these are formed. Encourage them to use different objects to make more shadows. Ask them to experiment with making shadows longer or shorter, experimenting with both the light source and the object.

Ask the children to work in pairs. Give each pair a torch so that they can create shadows. Ask them to find a way of using the torch to take the place of the Sun to create longer and shorter shadows. Can they explain why shadows are longer in the evening and in the morning than in the middle of the day? (The Sun is lower in the sky in the morning and evening.) Invite one pair to explain their findings.

History

Take the feely bag or box of concealed artefacts into the classroom. Invite individual children to come and feel inside the bag, describe (without seeing) what they can feel, extract the object and describe again. Discuss what each artefact might have been used for and when. Place in a visible position. Repeat the activity until all the objects are on display. Give everyone a piece of paper. Ask them to reproduce a timeline drawn by you on the flip chart (you can copy Figure 2 below) and to place each object in its approximate time on the line either by writing or drawing. Check the results together. Ask each child to make an observational drawing of one of the objects to be displayed on a classroom timeline.

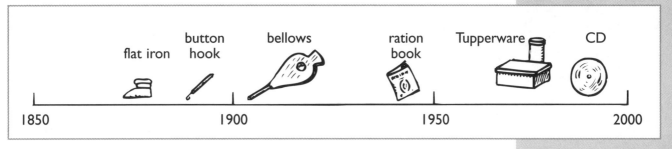

Figure 2

Music

Listen to a march (such as 'Onward Christian Soldiers'), a waltz ('O What a Wonderful Scene' from *Captain Noah and his Floating Zoo* (Horovitz)) and a lullaby ('Hush-a-Bye Baby'). Can the children hear the difference in the time? Explain that the time is the number of beats in a bar. Other hymns or suitable school songs could be used as examples. A taped version would be useful but a child singing could be just as effective.

Divide the children into small groups and give each group a time to work on a musical piece using the tuned and untuned instruments. Signature titles could be 'Walking with the Dinosaurs', 'Dancing with Prince Charming', 'Sleeping Child' or something that they think of themselves. Encourage them to perform to each other.

D&T

Think back with the children to the things Stig had in his cave (sticks, bottles, string, soil, water). How might they design an hour clock for Stig to tell the time? They might suggest sticks and the Sun, bottles and soil, water on a wheel, water dripping through holes and so on. Ask each child to design a timepiece, identifying the materials to use and drawing a series of diagrams to show how it would be assembled. Invite some children to explain to the class how their timepiece will function.

NOW OR LATER

■ Use the TV listings from a newspaper to discuss how long programmes are and the average times of programmes on one channel for a day. (mathematics)
■ Get the children to time each other, using a stopwatch, in track events such as 50 metres flat, 100 metres skipping. Can the children improve their performance times? (mathematics/PE)
■ Set up a discussion on the subject of wasting time. Make a list of the significant points to discuss the motion, *Sometimes it is important to waste time.* Invite the children to debate the subject and vote on the outcomes. (PSHE)

■ Talk about shadow clocks (sundials). Show how one can be made by fixing a circular piece of card to a south-facing wall or fence. Mark the card with the hours of daylight, 12 noon being at the bottom. Fasten a shadow stick to the top. Ask the children to plan and make a freestanding shadow clock. (D&T)

THE WHEEL

OBJECTIVES

■ writing for a purpose and from their own imagination **(English)**
■ measuring the circumference of a cylinder; recognising, measuring and naming angles **(mathematics)**
■ exploring and measuring fictional force **(science)**
■ recognising changes over a period of time **(history)**
■ appreciating the customs/ festivals of different religions **(RE)**
■ painting in the style of a famous artist **(art)**

RESOURCES

You will need:
■ paper, writing materials (English)
■ five cylindrical objects (coins, tins, cardboard rolls, plastic shapes and so on) for each pair of children, string, tape measure, strips of paper, white paper, coloured paper, compasses, protractors, rulers, scissors, glue (mathematics)
■ paper, toy vehicles; a flat-bottomed plastic container, string, sand and newton forcemeter for each group (science)
■ a wheel (such as a car tyre, a toy wheel or a bicycle wheel), reference books, CD-ROMs, access to computers and the Internet, paper, drawing and writing materials (history)
■ paper, writing materials (RE)
■ a print of Gainsborough's *The Market Cart* or Constable's *The Haywain* (available from Mainstone Publications, 01362 688395), watercolours, paper, brushes (art).

WHAT TO DO

English

Ask the children if any of them have been on a big wheel. How did they feel? What did they see? Ask them to imagine they are at the top of a big wheel and to describe objects and places from a bird's eye view looking down on the top of things. What catches their imagination? Encourage the class to compile a list of appropriate words to describe the scene.

In pairs, ask the children to use their imagination to describe to each other something which inspires them from the top of their imaginary wheel (for example, the shape of a river, the different colours of the roofs, hundreds of chimney pots, the dome or spire of a church, a maze of paths, tiny people and vehicles). Introduce the idea of writing a magazine article, encouraging people to experience the wheel ride. Ask each child to record their ideas in note form in preparation for writing the article. Leave some time for them to share their ideas.

Read 'Composed Upon Westminster Bridge' by William Wordsworth (see next page) to the children and discuss what they think Wordsworth saw as he leant over the bridge. Which of Wordsworth's descriptions impresses them most? How do they think a view of the Thames would differ from a big wheel? Many of the descriptions in the poem could be the same, for example, *the beauty of the morning; bright and glittering in the smokeless air; the river glideth.* Use these as examples to encourage the children to write phrases of their own, viewing the river from a great height. Ask the children to write their own imaginative description under the title 'A Bird's Eye View'. This could be poetry or prose and once completed should be shared.

Composed Upon Westminster Bridge
Earth has not anything to show more fair:
Dull would he be of soul who could pass by
A sight so touching in its majesty:
This city now doth, like a garment, wear
The beauty of the morning; silent, bare,
Ships, towers, domes, theatres, and temples lie
Open unto the fields, and to the sky;
All bright and glittering in the smokeless air.
Never did sun more beautifully steep
In his first splendour, valley, rock, or hill;
Ne'er saw I, never felt, a calm so deep!
The river glideth at his own sweet will:
Dear God! the very houses seem asleep;
And all that mighty heart is lying still!

Mathematics

Show the children the collection of cylindrical objects. Explain to the children that they are going to investigate the circumference of a circle. Discuss the meaning of *circumference* (the distance around the outside edge of the circle). Talk about how to measure the outside edge of a circle, noting that a ruler on its own is not a good idea because it is not flexible. A piece of string, a tape measure or strip of paper would be better because they would follow the curve of the cylinder. Show them that by marking a starting point on the circle and rolling it once all the way round along a strip of paper and marking the end will show the distance (see Figure 3). This can then be measured with a ruler.

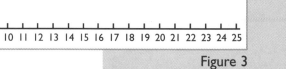

Figure 3

Give each pair of children the five cylindrical objects to measure using this rotating method. Once the end is marked, a strip of paper that length should be cut out and used to make a graph. A statement about these circumferences should accompany the graph.

Give each child two pieces of paper, a compass, a protractor, a ruler and some scissors. Refer back to their circle graphs. All the circles have different circumferences but there is one constant about them all. Do the children know what it is? (They all have 360° degrees.) Direct the discussion towards angles and remind them of the shape of a right angle. Do they know how many right angles there are in a circle? Can they measure a right angle by using the corner of their piece of paper and a protractor?

Encourage them to use the compass to draw as big a circle as possible on their piece of paper and then to use a pencil to mark the centre. Ask them to draw a line from the centre to the edge of the circle. Tell them to use a protractor to make a right angle and to cut it out. Next, ask them to draw an angle less than 90° and to cut this out also. Explain that this is an acute angle and that they are now left with an angle of more than 90°. Explain that this is an obtuse angle. Ask them to take all the shapes and glue them onto a piece of coloured paper, measure the angles and label them. Then tell them to add the measurements of the three angles together and write down the total (360°). To finish, ask the children to discuss any differences (for example, an acute angle is smaller than a right angle).

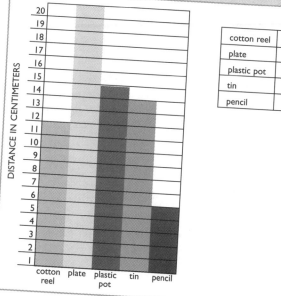

cotton reel	11cm
plate	20cm
plastic pot	14cm
tin	13cm
pencil	5cm

Figure 4

Ready to go! SUPPLY TEACHING

Science

Discuss with the children how a wheel turns on an axle so that it moves round and as it turns it comes into contact with the road surface causing friction. Use friction toys such as cars to illustrate frictional movement. Talk about how they work. Show the children a newton forcemeter with a small scale. Explain that one newton is the force which, acting on a mass of one kilogram, produces an acceleration of one metre per second.

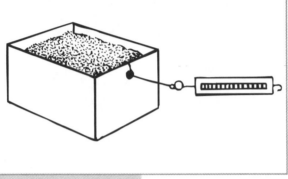

Figure 5

Give the children practice in reading the newtons on the forcemeter. Suggest that they discover the effect of friction for themselves. In groups of three, give each group a flat-bottomed plastic container, a piece of string, some sand and a newton meter. The children should weight the container with sand and tie one end of the string to the container and the other end to the newton meter (as in Figure 5).

One child from each group should pull the container along the floor by the newton meter, the second child should read the measurement and the third child should record the measurement on a chart. Once they have practised pulling and reading the measurement they can discover which surface gives the greatest resistance by pulling the container on different surfaces such as carpet, linoleum, wood or Perspex, or they could go outside pulling on tarmac, paving stones, concrete or gravel. In discussion, stress that the pull of the container along the surface is the force and the surface is the resistance.

History

Take a wheel into the classroom to show the children and to encourage a discussion about uses of the wheel. Lead them to think about life before the wheel and how the advent of the wheel changed the way of life for the human race. Give everyone the opportunity to research the history of the wheel for themselves using reference books, websites and CD-ROMs. Ask the children to draw a series of chronological pictures to show the development of the wheel and its use. Alongside or underneath each picture that they have drawn, ask them to write a detailed description of each of the wheels, indicating the approximate date, and highlighting the improvements that were made.

RE

Tell the children about different religions and encourage some children to talk about theirs. Explain that different religions have special festivals when people gather together. The year is like a wheel which has no end and no beginning. As it turns the seasons and festivals come round in a continuous circle like a wheel. Give the children the details in Figure 6, below, of some religious festivals and ask them to record important information in note form, on a sheet of A4 paper.

> ■ *Christian Festival – Easter* (March/April). This is a special time in the calendar when Christians remember that Jesus was crucified. This day is know as Good Friday. On the following Sunday, Easter Day, people celebrate Jesus rising from the dead. It is customary in many European countries for eggs to be decorated to symbolise new birth.
> ■ *Hindu Festival – Divali* (October/November). This is the most widely celebrated Hindu festival. Puja (worship) is offered to Lakshmi the goddess of good fortune. Lamps and candles are lit in people's homes to guide Lakshmi. The festival signifies the victory of light over darkness. Divali is also a Sikh festival celebrating the release of Guru Hargobind from prison.
> ■ *Chinese New Year* (January/February). This is a Buddhist Taoist festival. Each Chinese year is associated with twelve animal symbols. The New Year is a time when families reunite and gifts are given to children. Paper statues of the

kitchen god and protecting charms are displayed in the house. Good luck sayings are hung over the doorways.

■ *Jewish Festival – Hanukkah* (December). Hanukkah is known as the 'feast of lights' and celebrates the time when the Jews won the right to have their own temple and worship their own God. An eight-branched candlestick is lit for the festival, one candle burning on the first day, two on the second and so on for eight days.

■ *Harvest Festival* (September/October). This festival is customary in many religions. People express their thanks for the safe gathering of their particular harvest. Their harvest may be crops from the field, fish from the sea or minerals from the ground.

■ *Islamic Festival – Ramadan* (dates vary). This is a month of fasting when adult Muslims refrain from eating from dawn to sunset. They also try to read the whole of the Qur'an, the Muslim Holy Book, during this month. At the end of the month families share a special meal together.

■ *Buddha Day* (May/June). This is a time to remember the birth, enlightenment, death and teachings of Buddha and takes place on a full moon day. It is believed that Buddha attained enlightenment whilst meditating under a bodhi tree in Northern India. Here he gave his first sermon to a group of disciples and first taught the four Noble Truths and the Eightfold Path.

Art

Figure 6

Show the children the print of *The Market Cart* or *The Haywain*. Encourage them to look at the composition of the picture and make particular reference to the wheels. Encourage a discussion of the style of the painting, talking about the choice of colours, the shading and the composition. Ask the children how they think they could create the same effect. Using watercolour paints, give them the opportunity to paint in the style of the painter. A toy vehicle (tractor, car, lorry or cart) would be useful as part of the composition.

NOW OR LATER

■ Discuss the four points of the compass. Extend the children's knowledge to eight and then sixteen points. Ask them to devise a board game using these eight or sixteen points. (geography)

■ Throw a marble into a bowl of water to illustrate concentric circles. Ask the children to use a compass to draw some and then, using felt pens, draw different patterns within each circle. (art)

■ Show the children a picture of a big wheel at the fair or a picture of a water wheel. Ask them to experiment with construction kits to make a turning wheel. (D&T)

TRAVEL

RESOURCES

You will need:

■ travel brochures (enough for one between each pair), flip chart or board, pictures of holiday resorts, paper, writing materials, A3 paper, DTP programmes, access to computers (English)

■ photocopiable page 36, copies of local train timetables (mathematics)

■ flip chart or board, writing materials, paper (history)

■ a world map, small cards of place names to be found on the world map, a large map of Great Britain, flip chart or board (geography)

■ tuned and untuned instruments (xylophones, recorders, tambourines, woodblocks and so on), tape recorder, blank tape (music)

■ paper, writing materials (D&T).

OBJECTIVES

■ scanning texts for information; writing for a purpose **(English)**

■ understanding averages and how to calculate them **(mathematics)**

■ comparing past and present travel **(history)**

■ recognising how places fit within a wider geographical context **(geography)**

■ improvising and developing musical ideas **(music)**

■ designing footwear **(D&T)**

WHAT TO DO

English

Take into the classroom the selection of travel brochures so that there is at least one for each pair of children to look at. Invite the children to browse through them for a limited time. Ask the children to identify the area that they have been looking at (country, region), what kind of accommodation (hotel, self-catering), the facilities of the resort (organised tours, talks) and so on. Write headings on the flip chart for all to see (location and area, accommodation, facilities) and invite them to give you associated words (Greece, countryside, mountains, hotel, room service, tours

available). The children could provide these words either from the brochure or use suggestions of their own. Write their words beneath each heading.

Using the suggested word lists, ask them to write their own paragraph for an imaginary holiday, focusing on just one of the sections (location and area, accommodation or facilities). Some children could read theirs to the class while others should be encouraged to make positive suggestions for redrafting.

Divide the children into groups of four and give them a picture cut out from a travel brochure or magazine showing a holiday place. Ask the groups to discuss the picture, focusing on where they think the place is (for example, which continent), what the weather might be like (hot or cold climate), if there is an indication in the picture of the kind of accommodation (hotel, self-catering, camping) and so on.

Ask the groups to talk about their picture to the whole class. Give them the headings again and ask each member of the group to decide which part they would like to write about. The final aim of each group is to present, on A3 paper, an inviting description of the resort shown in the picture in the same format as the travel brochure. If possible, some children could produce their brochures on the computer using a DTP programme. Display the final results.

Mathematics

Give each child a copy of photocopiable page 36, which shows the temperatures and the hours of sunshine at a holiday destination. Encourage them to talk together about what the various numbers, lines and symbols represent, for example how hot, how cold, hours of sunshine per day, differences between July and August and so on. Can the children offer suggestions as to how the average temperature for the month was calculated? (The daily temperatures added together and divided by days of the month.) Give them some simple examples to try for a week (26°C, 24°C, 30°C, 29°C, 27°C, 27°C, 26°C). Encourage them to add these together and divide by seven. They should find the average of these seven temperature is 27°C. Direct the children back to photocopiable page 36, and ask them to calculate the average temperature for the year and the average amount of sunshine and check their answers together.

Talk with the children about how they travel to school and how long they estimate it takes them to get there. Choose six children with different travelling times and draw a chart on the flip chart showing these in relation to each other. Can the children remember how they could find the average travelling time using these given times? (Add together the six times and divide by six.) Give another example: *A bus travels to the swimming baths each day of the week. It takes a slightly different route each time (20 minutes, 18 minutes, 19 minutes, 25 minutes, 28 minutes).* Can the children work out the average time it takes? (22 minutes.)

Give the children a local train timetable. Ask them to work out the average time of the trains between two destinations for each day. Give everyone a chance to check their answers.

History

Ask the children how they might travel to their holiday destinations (bus, car, plane or train). Do they enjoy the travelling part of the holiday? How do they think their parents travelled to holidays in their youth? What about their grandparents or their great-grandparents? Explain that in their great, great-grandparents' time (Victorian times) there was very limited travel and only the wealthy people went very far. Can they suggest how the rich travelled (coaches and horses) and how the poor travelled (stage coach, walking)? What made all the difference to holiday travel? Emphasise that the train especially made a big difference to travel in the 19th century as train tracks were laid to the seasides in Britain and the mass of people, for the first time, were able to travel there.

Read the poem *The song the train sang* (below) by Neil Adams to create the excitement of steam train travel. If there are pictures of steam trains available, show them to the children. Ask: *What would it have been like to travel on a steam train?* (Dusty, sooty, smelly, smoky, noisy.) Divide the class into groups for a short discussion of travel in this way. To encourage further discussion, set up a debate to discuss the statement: *Travel on a steam train in Victorian Britain was better than travel today.* Write the statement on a flip chart and encourage a lively discussion, keeping a record of the main points raised. Take a final vote to see the outcome of the debate.

The song the train sang
Now
When the
Steam hisses
Now
When the
Coupling clashes;
Now
When the
Wind rushes
Comes the slow but sudden swaying,
Every truck and carriage trying
For a smooth and better rhythm
For a smooth and singing rhythm
This… is… the… one
That… is… the… one
This is the one, that is the one
This is the one, that is the one
Over the river, past the mill,
Through the tunnel, over the hill;
Round the corner, past the wall
Through the woods where the trees grow tall.
Then in sight of the town by the river
Brake by the crossing where the white leaves quiver.
Slow as the streets of the town slide past
And windows stare at the jerking of the coaches
Coming into the station approaches
Stop at the front
Stop at the front
Stop… at the front
Stop… at the
Stop.
AHHHHH!

Geography

Use a classroom-sized map displayed for all to see and ask different children to point out where they went, or where someone they know went to on holiday. Do they know where certain countries are? Have a general discussion about what the map shows (continents, countries, seas, oceans, capitals) and how easy it is to travel these days.

Place all of the place name cards in a hat or bag, and ask the children to take one each at random and, using Blu-Tack or the equivalent, place the name in position on the world map. Is it in the correct place?

Display a large map of Great Britain for the children to identify places one can travel to from London. They may need to be reminded of the directions north, south, east and west and use either the wall map or individual atlases. Write a list of well-known places (Glasgow, Manchester, Birmingham, Dover) on the flip chart and ask them to point these places out on the map and to say in which direction they would need to travel to get there from London.

Music

The class will need to be divided into small groups for this activity and both tuned (any instrument that can play a tune such as a xylophone) and untuned (those which only play rhythms such as wood blocks) instruments made available.

Talk to the children about the River Thames in London and some of the places they might visit as they travel along it on a sightseeing boat. Each group should be given one of the famous sights or they can choose one themselves (Tower of London, London Eye, Tower Bridge and so on). Encourage them to make up a piece of music that includes some of the sounds they might hear there (children's voices, bells, traffic, tour guides, water, music and so on). One group will need to be the people in the boat. It would make a contrasting sound if this group only used their voices, repeating phrases tourists might make when they are looking at important landmarks. The subject will change according to where they are on the journey. Use the conductor (who can be one of the children) to point to each group as the sightseers arrive at their sight and intersperse each new sight with the vocal group. Record the results so the children can hear what they have created.

D&T

Remind yourself of where the children have said they like to go on holidays, directing the discussion towards locations (seaside, mountains, places of interest). Ask them to decide which footwear would be the most appropriate for their choice of location. (For example, trainers for sporting comfort, sandals for cool and comfortable wear, walking shoes for hiking and support.) Focus on the sandal, a common form of travel footwear and together establish the criteria that would be considered if they were designing and making a sandal to wear while travelling in a hot country. (For example, strong, securely fastened, open on the top of the foot, solid under the foot.) Display the list of criteria for all to see and then ask the children which materials would be most appropriate, what kind of glue might be needed to make sure they were firmly made. The children should then design their own sandal.

NOW OR LATER

■ Invite the children to research a well-known expedition such as Hillary's Everest expedition or Scott's Antarctic journey, using relevant websites. (ICT)
■ Listen together to some of the music written by famous composers relating to journeys. For example, *The Planets Suite* by Gustav Holst, Mendelssohn's *Fingal's Cave*, *The Little Train of the Caipira* by Villa Lobos. Encourage the children to listen and imagine what might be happening and to retell the tale in their own words. (music)
■ Ask the children to make a list of some of the things used in travelling (suitcase, passport, sandals, sunglasses, and so on). Then encourage them to draw and cut out these objects and make a travel collage. (art)
■ Ask the children to try to make the sandal that they designed in D&T. (D&T)

A medieval market

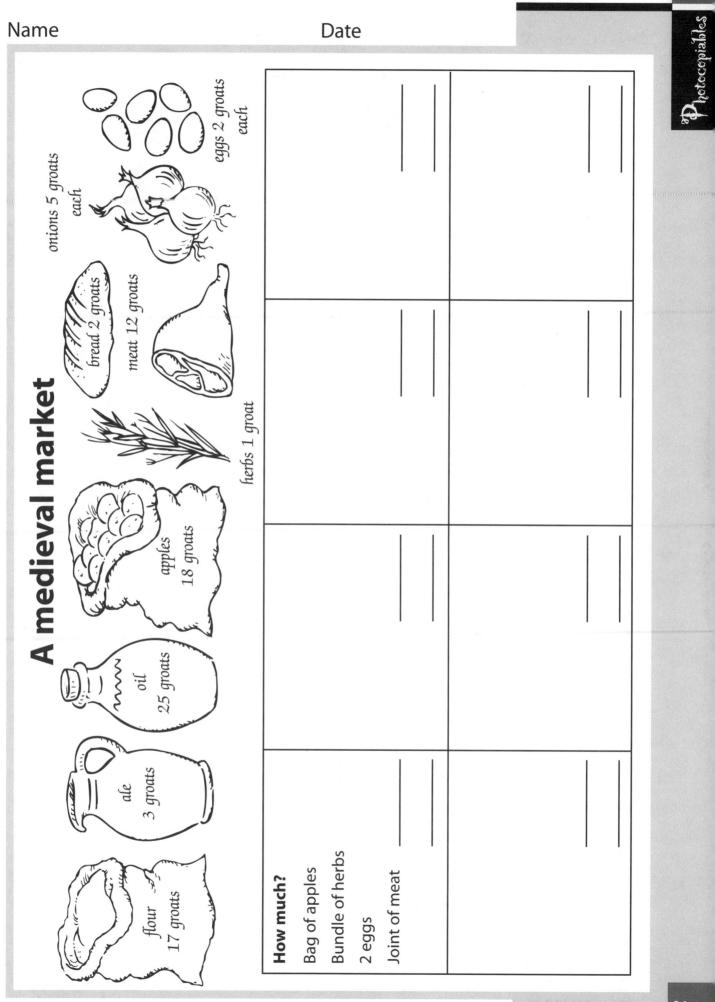

onions 5 groats each

eggs 2 groats each

bread 2 groats

meat 12 groats

herbs 1 groat

apples 18 groats

oil 25 groats

ale 3 groats

flour 17 groats

How much?

Bag of apples

Bundle of herbs

2 eggs

Joint of meat

Ready to go! SUPPLY TEACHING

Photocopiables

Going to market

side of 1 square = 2 kilometres

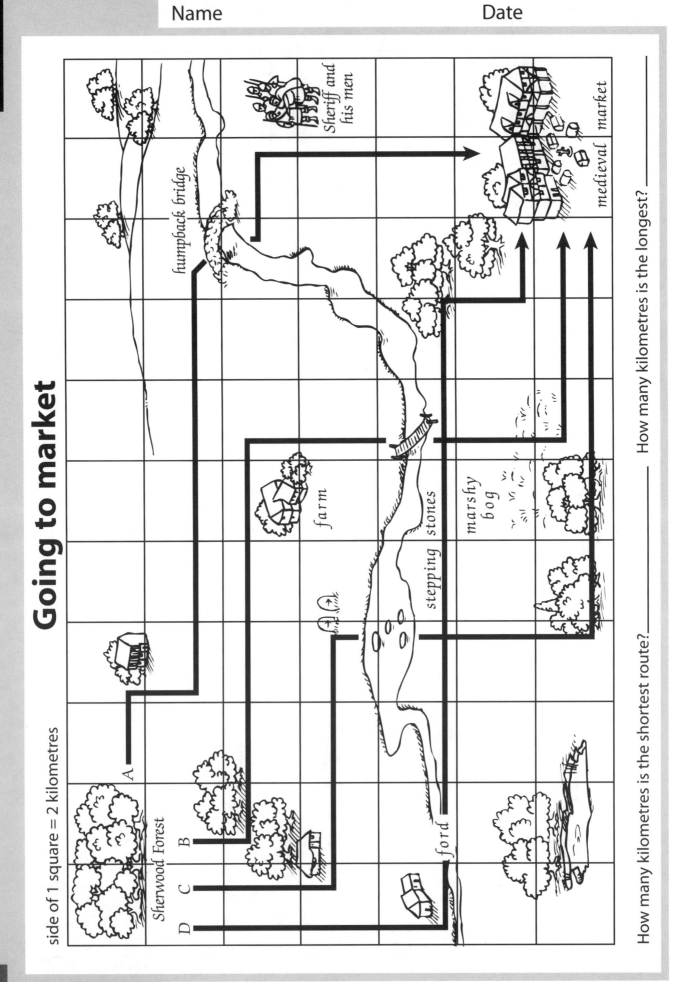

How many kilometres is the shortest route? _____

How many kilometres is the longest? _____

Water levels – River Severn

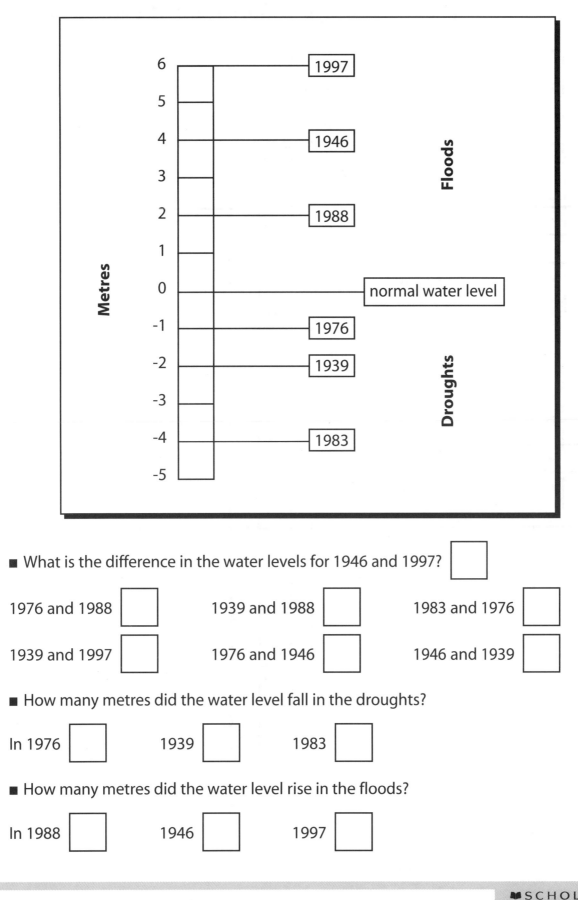

- What is the difference in the water levels for 1946 and 1997? ☐

1976 and 1988 ☐ 1939 and 1988 ☐ 1983 and 1976 ☐

1939 and 1997 ☐ 1976 and 1946 ☐ 1946 and 1939 ☐

- How many metres did the water level fall in the droughts?

In 1976 ☐ 1939 ☐ 1983 ☐

- How many metres did the water level rise in the floods?

In 1988 ☐ 1946 ☐ 1997 ☐

Draw a line

Draw a line	How much do you think?
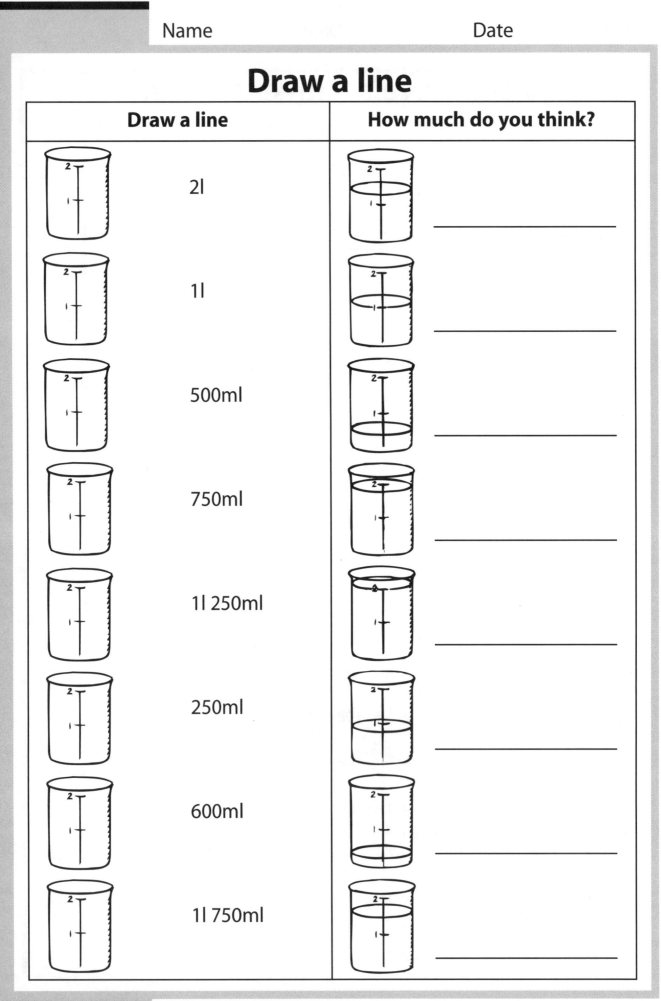 2l	_____
1l	_____
500ml	_____
750ml	_____
1l 250ml	_____
250ml	_____
600ml	_____
1l 750ml	_____

Ready to go! SUPPLY TEACHING

Train timetable

	Departure	Arrival
Shrewsbury to Derby	09.25 11.44 14.58 16.12	11.45 14.09 17.25 18.36
Shrewsbury to Edinburgh	07.06 10.55 15.33 17.49	12.10 15.50 20.36 23.03
Shrewsbury to York	07.34 09.27 13.53 16.42	11.04 12.50 17.28 20.15
Shrewsbury to Chester	08.31 12.38 15.54 18.16	09.27 13.44 16.51 17.20

Average temperatures in Majorca

- How were the average monthly temperatures calculated?
- What do the symbols mean?
- Which is the hottest month?
- Which is the coolest month?
- How were the average hours of sunshine calculated for each month?
- Work out the average temperature for the year.
- What is the average sun for the year?

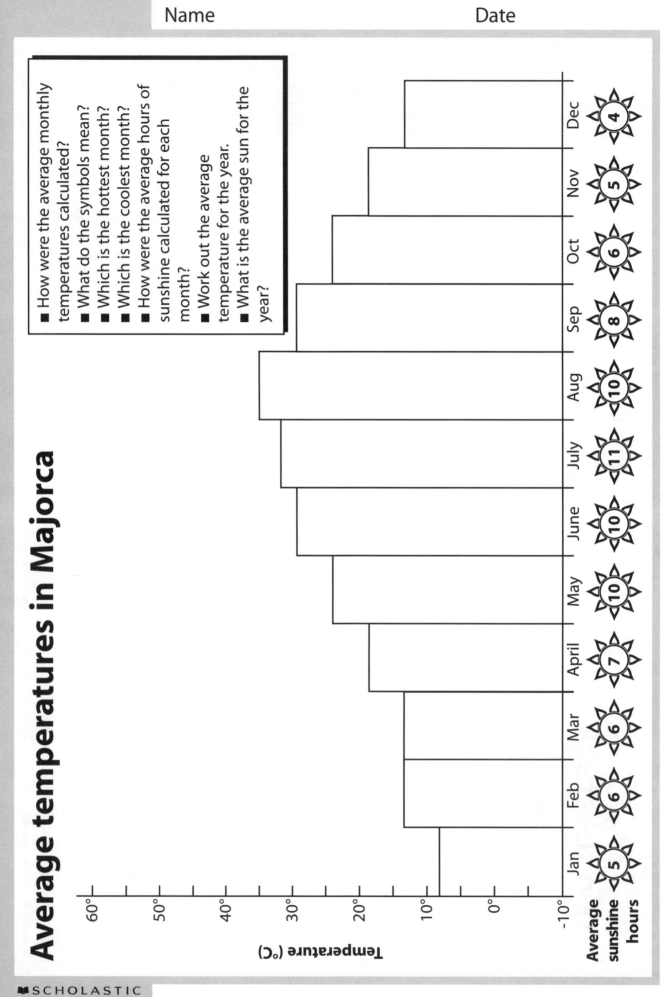

Temperature (°C)

	Jan	Feb	Mar	April	May	June	July	Aug	Sep	Oct	Nov	Dec
Average sunshine hours	5	6	6	7	10	10	11	10	8	6	5	4

This section provides a wide variety of cross-curricular activities for five-day cover on the themes of Living things, Measures, Shakespeare's land and Sunny islands.

LIVING THINGS

RESOURCES

You will need:

■ photocopiable page 59, a packet of seeds, mime cards each showing an *-ing* word (verbs), paper, writing materials (English)

■ photocopiable page 60, paper, writing materials, different-sized leaves/flowers, six different-sized cereal packets, graph paper, seed packets, flip chart or board (mathematics)

■ white flowers or plants, food colouring, water, containers (science)

■ a bottle of beer, loaf of bread, map of the Nile Delta (history)

■ paper, writing materials, tuned and untuned instruments, tape recorder, blank tape (RE/music)

■ blank, plain postcards (for making notes) for each child, writing materials (PSHE)

■ a pencil or paint drawing of a dandelion, plants for the children to draw, pen, ink, magnifying glass and white cartridge paper for each child (art)

■ paper, writing materials (D&T)

■ tape player and tape recorded in RE/music (PE).

WHAT TO DO

English

Ask the children to imagine they are in the bakery department of a supermarket and can see a lot of different kinds of bread. Can they name any of them? (For example, bloomer, plait, bagel.) Explain that a word that tells you the name of a person, place or thing is called a noun, and if it is a special name (for example 'Mary'), then this is a proper noun.

As a class, collect nouns, for example lists of fruit and vegetables. Then, read through the first two verses of 'I wandered lonely as a cloud' by William Wordsworth (below) together and then ask the children to think about the nouns within it. Read it again slowly, asking them to make a note of any nouns that they hear.

I wandered lonely as a cloud
That floats on high, o'er vales and hills
When all at once I saw a crowd
A host of golden daffodils
Beside the lake, beneath the trees
Fluttering and dancing in the breeze.

Continuous as the stars that shine
And twinkle on the milky way,
They stretched in never ending line
Along the margin of the bay.
Ten thousand saw I at a glance
Tossing their heads in sprightly dance.

Take a packet of seeds into the classroom and ask the children to describe the packet (colourful, informative, bright, attractive). Point out that the words they are

OBJECTIVES

■ developing knowledge of word classification **(English)**
■ reading and drawing graphs and pie charts **(mathematics)**
■ creating experiments to show that water is transported through the stem to other parts of a plant **(science)**
■ comparing breadmaking in different periods **(history)**
■ debating local environmental issues **(geography)**
■ comparing creation stories **(RE)**
■ creating music and movement in response to a piece of text **(music/PE)**
■ preparing a talk on caring for a plant or animal **(PSHE)**
■ drawing a plant accurately and in detail **(art)**
■ designing a growing box for a plant **(D&T)**

using are adjectives (words that give nouns more information). For instance, a *blossoming* tree is very different from a *dead* tree and a *rosy, red* apple very different from a *rotting* apple. Create some pairs together that contrast with each other and give the children an opportunity to write some for themselves.

As a class, look at the passage on photocopiable page 59, 'Colour in the garden', and ask the children to find all the adjectives there and write them down. Some children will be able to use these in sentences of their own.

Do the children know that verbs are words that make pictures move and bring nouns to life? Bring out the mime cards each showing an *-ing* verb, give one to each child and ask them to mime the word. Who can guess what the verb is?

At the beginning of a session, take on a particular mood (grumpily, haughtily, sadly) as you speak, talking to the children about some of the work on a previous day. Once you have finished, ask them to tell you how they think you were speaking. Encourage words ending in *-ly* as observations, then explain that many adverbs can be formed from adjectives by adding *-ly*. Adverbs give you information about the verb, they 'add' to it.

Describe to the children a scene in a marketplace of busy stallholders selling their wares and anxious shoppers hurrying to buy. Tell the children that they are required by the local newspaper to write a descriptive piece of writing about the scene (you could use the scenarios suggested below to help get the children started). Give the children a list of adverbs as shown in the box and tell them they must use all the adverbs provided. Encourage them to use more of their own. Hear a selection of the writings and identify the adverbs together.

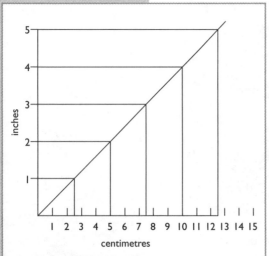

Figure 7

Market scenarios bargaining; being given wrong change; helping an old lady
Adverbs happily; sadly; grumpily; willingly; hopefully: gratefully; anxiously

---

Build up a chart of word classification on the flip chart with the children, recapping as you go along on the work done earlier. Refer to Figure 7 which shows how a language tree can be built, and ask the children to create one of their own, using a different starting word. Hear some of these.

Mathematics

Discuss with the children how all living things need food. Ask them where they would like to eat out if given a choice – a burger bar, pizza restaurant, fish and chip shop or supermarket cafe? Make a tally chart on the flip chart to show the results. Ask the children to look at photocopiable page 60 which shows a pie chart of the results of a 'What you eat' survey. What does this tell the children? (Burgers are the most popular.) Which is the least popular? Ask them to write a statement about this and then use the findings of the class tally chart to draw an approximate representation on the lower circle. If a data-handling programme is available then this could be used.

Take into the classroom either the different-sized leaves or flowers with stems. In small groups or with the whole class, measure the stems or leaves in centimetres and keep a record of the results. Copy Figure 8, which shows a conversion graph, onto the flip chart. Explain that by finding the correct measurement in centimetres, the children should be able to find the measurement in inches by following the appropriate lines. Ask them to convert their measurements into inches.

Display the six cereal packets and ask six children to measure the heights. Make a chart on the flip chart of the height of the

Figure 8

packets in centimetres. Explain to the children that because the measurements are so large, you would like them to devise a scale to reduce them. Ask for suggestions as to how this can be done. (For example, use 1 square for 2cm.) Ask them to draw a block graph showing this representation for the cereal packets and to write a statement about it.

Look at the seed packets together, paying particular attention to the approximate heights of the flowers. (For example, cosmos – 91cm, marigold – 22cm.) Discuss the difference between the tallest and the shortest flower and ask the children to suggest a suitable scale to represent them. Given this information they should be able to draw a block graph. Ask them to explain their choice of scale in writing.

Science

Divide the class into small groups, each with the white flower or plant, food colouring, containers and water. Ask each group to discuss what they could do with these objects to create an experiment to show that a plant is a living thing. Encourage them to record this on paper and make a note of the plant on that day and what they think will happen to it during the week. Expect them to put the plant in the container with the water and food colouring, predicting that the veins of the plant will change colour. Place the experiments in a safe but visible position for the rest of the week.

Towards the end of the week when changes can be observed, continue the work about plant life. Discuss together the parts of the plant (roots, stem, leaves, flower) and talk about the role each plays in the life of the plant (roots taking the moisture and food from the soil and giving support, stem taking the water to the leaves, leaves making food for the plant by photosynthesis and the flowers producing seeds for reproducing new plants). Look at the most successful of the children's experiments and discuss what has been happening.

History

Give each child a small piece of bread to taste and ask if they can identify any of the ingredients in it (flour, water, yeast, salt, sugar). Can anyone tell you how bread is made today (with machines in bakeries)? Explain to the children that bread formed part of the Ancient Egyptians' staple diet and that they needed to grow different kinds of grain, emmer (a type of wheat) and barley to make it with. The children will need to know where Egypt is and a map of the Nile Delta would be useful. Show the map and ask them where they think the wheat and barley would have been grown. (The River Nile's banks after the floods had subsided and a mud bank was revealed.) What kind of weather do they think the Egyptians had? (Very hot and sunny with a short rainy season, or inundation, between July and October.)

Ask the children if they think that bread would have looked and tasted the same in the time of Ancient Egypt as it does now (it would have been flatter as they did not use yeast). Can anyone suggest how the Egyptians might have made their bread? Explain how they prepared their grain by crushing it between two stones, shaking the husks away and then sifting out the insects and chipped bits of the stones before mixing it with water.

Invite the children to imagine they are living in Ancient Egypt and to create a recipe for an Egyptian loaf of bread. The recipe should include ingredients, a method and the equipment they would need to make the bread.

Geography

Choose a local environmental issue if possible, for example, building a housing estate on a popular site, replacing woodland with a motorway or placing a landfill site next to a beauty spot. If this is not possible then pose a question or debating statement to the whole class such as, *Why are there so many urban foxes?*, *Why are the beaches no longer clean to walk on?* or *The school hedge should not be removed to enlarge the playground*. Ask the children to think what their opinions are on the issue and to state them to the class clearly. At the end of the session take a vote on the motion.

RE/Music

Read through the following creation stories from major religions, then ask the children to record the similarities and differences.

Jews/Christians

In the beginning there was a big, black empty space. God created:

- Day 1 – Light and dark
- Day 2 – Water
- Day 3 – Sea/land/plants/trees
- Day 4 – Sun/moon/stars
- Day 5 – Birds/fish
- Day 6 – Animals/man
- Day 7 – Rest day

Muslims

God says 'Be' and the thing he wants will appear – Heaven, Earth, animals, birds, fish, sun, moon, stars, angels, rain for plants to grow. The angels were sent to Earth to bring back seven handfuls of earth. From these, God made Adam.

Hindus

The world has been made and destroyed many times. This will happen again. The Supreme God is Brahman. Brahma, Vishnu and Shiva are different forms of Brahman. Brahma makes the world and all things on it. Vishnu looks after the world when Brahma sleeps. Shiva destroys the world. Brahma wakes and makes the world again.

Divide the class into six small groups, giving each group a selection of both tuned and untuned instruments. Allocate different religions and stages of the creation to each group to work on. Suggest to the children that they discuss as a group their creation's stage before they begin to create music to describe it. Will the music be loud or soft, high or low, have short notes or long notes? Do they need to keep a record of their sounds in graphic notation (picture form)? Will they need a conductor to keep them all together? Once they have a musical plan they should begin to put their ideas together. Listen to each group as they play their musical pieces and once all the groups are ready, ask them to play them to each other. Tape the end result for future use.

PSHE

Invite all of the children to prepare a one-minute talk on their favourite plant or animal. They must include a clear description, a reason for choosing the animal or plant and the ways in which they care for it. Give them a postcard or something of similar size to write notes from which to speak and invite a selection to deliver their thoughts to the whole class. Lead the discussion toward general care and respect for all people, plants and animals.

Art

Look together at a pencil or paint drawing of a dandelion (it could be one of your own). There is a very good one in the Philip Green Art Pack (contact Galt on 0161 428 9111). Ask the children to notice how the plant is represented through art. Give everyone the opportunity to recreate on paper either the plants used for the science experiment, showing the details of the veins in the plant, or a different set of plants. Ask the children to use a magnifying glass to look carefully at the detail of the plant before drawing with pen and ink on white cartridge paper.

D&T

The main focus of this activity is for the children to design a growing box. First they will need to discuss what it is that living things need for healthy growth (light, warmth, water, nutrients). Ask them what they would need to make this box (transparent material, water and waterproof material, a place to stand the box, the dimensions needed for the box to sit comfortably in its place, soil or compost and so on). They should design the box giving all the relevant measurements and requirements.

PE

Use the taped sections from RE/Music above as a starting point for this work. Divide the class into six small groups, giving each group one section of the music. Encourage growth movements in all the sections to correspond with the growing sounds, the dynamics of the music. Observe each group as they are working and give helpful comments to enhance the work.

NOW OR LATER

■ Develop the children's knowledge of word classification further by asking them to use adjectives in poetry writing about woodlands, meadows and so on. (English)
■ Create an experiment to show how plants need light for healthy growth, by covering one part of a leaf and noting the changes in colour. (science)
■ Ask the children to use a PE hoop to mark out a section of grassland or a place under a hedgerow to make a survey of all the plant life they can find there. (science)
■ Encourage the children to look at how our diet has changed over the past few years, in particular how it has changed since the last war. Ask: *How were growing conditions different then? How have our needs changed and why?* (history)

MEASURES

RESOURCES

You will need:
■ paper, writing materials, dictionaries and thesauruses, flip chart or board, local newspaper (English)
■ several different-sized boxes (such as cereal boxes and shoe boxes) and multilink cubes, A4 sheets of paper for each child, boxes of sand, rice or pasta and sets of scales for each group table, 24 multi-building cubes for each child, rulers for each child, paper, writing materials (mathematics)
■ one very large sheet of paper and body part labels ('heart', 'lungs', 'stomach' and so on) for each group, paper, writing materials, stopwatches for each pair of children (science)

OBJECTIVES

■ looking at rhyme; using dictionaries and thesauruses; understanding words have different shades of meanings **(English)**
■ understanding volume and capacity **(mathematics)**
■ observing the effect of exercise and rest on breathing and pulse **(science)**

OBJECTIVES (CONT)

- looking at transport and exploration in a past society **(history)**
- showing how scale is used in map reading **(geography)**
- discovering accurate measurements in the Bible; caring for our world **(RE)**
- using musical measures to create rhythms **(music)**
- painting in the style of a particular artist **(art)**
- designing and making a gift carrier **(D&T)**
- measuring distance and speed accurately **(PE)**

- photocopiable page 61, a birthday card (see activity for more details), paper, writing materials (history)
- local Ordnance Survey map, squared paper for each child, writing materials (geography)
- musical flash cards (see Figure 10), a selection of tuned and untuned instruments (music)
- artwork by Clarice Cliff, A4 paper and paints for each child (art)
- paper, writing materials (D&T)
- a whistle, variety of balls (PE).

WHAT TO DO

English

Read to the children this account of life in 1945, as told by a child of the time.

> 'As a child in 1945, things were very different from today. Every morning the milk cart would come trundling along the road, with its churns of milk rattling against the wooden boards. We used to run out into the road taking with us a pottery, quart jug for the milk. The milkman would use his 1 pint ladle and pour 2 pints into our jug, out of his 10 gallon churn. On our way home from school, Mum would stop at the bakery to buy a 2lb tin loaf, and we used to eat the crusts as we were walking back. It was wrapped in tissue paper and had a delicious smell.'

Have any of the children heard their grandparents or great-grandparents talking about life at this time? Ask them to retell some of the stories. What do they think is so different about life then and now? Focus on the weights and measurements which have changed completely. Do they think that things have changed for the better or the worse? They could record some of their thoughts in a now and then chart in either pictures or words.

Read the following extract from *The Magic Pudding* by Norman Lindsay to the class.

> Take my advice, don't carry bags,
> For bags are just as bad as swags;
> They're never made to measure.
> To see the world, your simple trick
> Is but to take a walking stick –
> Assume an air of pleasure,
> And tell the people near and far
> You stroll about because you are
> A Gentleman of Leisure.

On a second reading, emphasise the rhyming words for *measure*. Discuss how the poet has used these at regular intervals in the verse (lines 3, 6 and 12). Can the children think of any other words that would rhyme with *measure* (*treasure*, *pressure*)? There are very few. For a word such as *rhyme* there are many more, (*time, crime, lime, dime, grime*). Encourage the children to try the -*ime* sound with each letter of the alphabet to see which words they can find. Ask them to write these words in alphabetical order and then do the same with words with -*ate* sounds (*bait, crate, date, fate, great, hate*) and -*tion* words, (*action, bastion, creation, duration*). The children can then use one of these lists as a starting point for a 12-line poem (stanza) which has lines 1 and 2, 4 and 5, 7 and 8 and 10 and 11 rhyming, and lines 3, 6, 9 and 12 having a different rhyme. Listen to some of these.

Every child will need to have access to a dictionary and a thesaurus. Have a quick look at each together and give the children some words to find. For example, ask them to find the word *mark*. What meanings do they come up with? Then ask them to find meanings for the words *size* then *estimate* and then *gauge*. Each answer should refer back to the word *measure*. Explain to the children that words can have several meanings and that these can be found in a complete dictionary. A thesaurus will give some of the different meanings of words. Ask the children to look up *measure* and see which words are shown. They could then write a few sentences to show that they understand the different meanings of the words.

On the flip chart, write out the following sentences, some 'Did you know' statements. All are statements including measurements and these are correct, but there is one spelling mistake, one grammatical mistake and one punctuation mistake in each. Can they find them and write the sentence correctly? They should be encouraged to use the dictionary. Leave time to check the results.

1. Sir Edmund Hillary and Sherpa Tenzing shaked hands at the hihest point in the world at 11.30am on 29 May 1953?
2. Thai snake kite were 24 times' longer than one of the longest dinosores, Diplodocus.
3. A starfish usualy has five arms. but it do have between four and fifty?
4. The greatest tides happens in the Bay of Fundy, Canada. They can rise above fifteen metres, higher than a four storey biulding in six hours.
5. The best surfing waves is up to nine metres high and occur in Hawaii. Australia and Bali?
6. One, sandcastle contain millions of grains of sand?

Explain to the children that they are going to measure or mark columns on their paper in the same way that a newspaper editor measures columns for newsprint. Show them a local newspaper and look together at the way different pages are marked out. Choose a topical local issue (a collapsing building, a lorry stuck under a bridge and so on) and invite the children, on A4-sized paper, to mark out the layout of their page to include the headline, byline, text and a picture. They should all try to produce one page of news and the results could be displayed.

Mathematics

Take into the classroom the different-sized boxes and show the children one multilink cube. Can the children guess how many cubes might fit into one of the boxes? Fill the box and see whose estimate was correct. Try the same with two boxes that have a different shape but that have the same volume inside. (You will need to check this beforehand.) Explain to them that the space inside an object can be the same even when the outside looks completely different. Divide the class into small groups, each with a selection of boxes and multilink cubes to calculate as accurately as possible the volume of each. These should be recorded and discussed.

Give each child a sheet of A4 paper. Ask them to make one four-sided open box (see Figure 9). They should measure and draw diagonally from each corner a line of any size and then cut along these lines. The sides will need to be folded and then the corners safely glued in place. The boxes should all look different. Place on each group table the sand, rice or pasta for the children to fill their box. Each child in a group will need to have the same filling. Ask each child to weigh their filling and then record both their own and the other members of the group's findings on a chart and where possible record the results on a bar chart. The results should show that the boxes all have the same capacity.

Figure 9

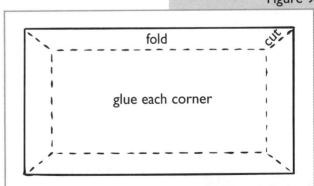

fold
cut
glue each corner

43

Give each child or pair of children 24 multilink cubes to make individual models of their choice using all the cubes. When they are complete, compare the shapes and the sizes of the models, showing that the volume is the same (24 cubes). Change the number of cubes, and ask the children in pairs to make three separate models using different numbers of cubes. Ask: *Which has the greater, the lesser, the same volume?* Ask them to draw and record these results (the net of the shapes) on squared paper, with each square representing one cube showing that the volume is different in each case.

Tell the children to find objects in and around the classroom that are cubes or cuboid shape to measure (empty boxes, building blocks, pencil boxes, lunch boxes). The length, breadth and height of these should be measured to the nearest centimetre and the volume calculated by multiplying length by breadth by height. The final answer will be in cubic centimetres. These measurements should be recorded and then ordered, starting at the smallest. The final measurements could be recorded on a block graph.

Science

Divide the class into small groups, giving each group a large sheet of paper and ask the children to draw round the smallest child. Present each group with the labels, 'heart', 'lungs', 'stomach', 'intestine' and 'kidneys' and ask the group members to identify and place the labels on the correct parts of the body. Check that the children have these in the correct positions.

The main focus will then be on the heart and the lungs, so make a point of showing the children exactly where they are. Tell the children they are going to measure both heart beats and breath rates, working with a partner. *Does anyone know how to find a pulse? What does the pulse tell you?* The best pulse beat will be found on the inside of the left wrist, below the thumb using the first and second finger tips of the other hand to feel it. Another place is the neck and a third point is the temple of the head. Give each pair of children a stopwatch to measure the pulse rate of their partner and to record it for one minute. The children should be resting when the first rate is taken and active when the second rate is taken. Ask: *What is the difference?* Reinforce the difference by introducing other activities (skipping, running, jumping). Once the pulse rates are recorded, ask the children to notice the breathing pattern of their partner, both in a relaxed situation and in an active situation. These rates should also be recorded and compared with other pairs. Explain that the heart pumps the blood to the lungs, where it picks up the oxygen it needs, then it goes back to the heart which pumps it around the body to provide the needed oxygen there.

History

Have a birthday card prepared, addressed to King Hoaken of Norway with this message written on it:

Congratulations on your 75th birthday. We have arrived.
Best wishes to you.
The Kon Tiki expedition.

Have any of the children any ideas from whom this message came? Tell them that in 1947 Thor Heyerdahl, a Norwegian, decided to sail on a primitive raft from South America to Polynesia (Hawaii, Fiji, Samoa, and Tonga) to prove that it had previously been done in AD500. He set out with five of his companions to build a raft in the same style, using mainly balsa wood, and he called the raft Kon Tiki. People were sceptical about his claims because they thought that he wouldn't be able to steer it through the high seas and that water would penetrate the logs and sink it. He proved his point by completing the journey and then sent the king the message. Obviously the raft had to be built to exact measurements for the journey to succeed and these are shown on photocopiable page 61. It was the kind of raft used by the South American Indians in the 15th century.

Have a look at the photocopiable page with the children and discuss how it might have been made. Ask the children: *Where would they find the materials? Which part would have been built first? What about stability and safety? Where would the crew eat and sleep?* Would the children like to have been on the raft? Remind them of some of the difficulties and dangers. (For example, sharks, high seas, strong currents, coral reefs, weather, high winds.) Invite them to write two paragraphs on the photocopiable sheet about building the raft and living on the raft. Ask some of the children to read them to the whole class.

Geography
You will need a local Ordnance Survey map (small scale), enlarged to enable the children to see how the map can represent their area. The measurements on these maps have to be extremely accurate. Ask them to select a small section (3 x 3 squares) of an interesting part of the map. The aim is for the children to enlarge the map by increasing the scale. How will they do this? They could use a new scale of two squares for one square. The larger representation should also show the features shown on the original map (telephone, church, tent and so on).

RE
Another person who built a boat to exact measurements, was Noah, whose story is often told to both the Jews and the Christians, and can be found in the book of Genesis, in the Bible. After God created the earth and everything in it, the Christians and the Jews believed that God was very angry with the people. They were not taking care of the land and they were spending a lot of time arguing and fighting. He was so cross that he decided to send a flood and the only person to be given warning was Noah. Noah was told to build a special boat, called an ark, and to take onto it all of his family and two of each kind of animal. God gave Noah specific and very clear instructions.

The older versions of the story have the measurements given in *cubits*. A *cubit* was an old measure which meant the length of the arm from the elbow to the tip of the middle finger. It was about 18–22in or 46–56cm. The ark was to be 300 cubits long, 50 cubits wide and 30 cubits high. Can the children calculate the size in centimetres? (Newer versions of the Bible have this measurement.) Some children might like to calculate the volume of the ark.

Figure 10

The boat was built, and everyone stayed on it for 40 days until it stopped raining. Then they left the ark and began new lives. What kinds of things do the children think we are doing in our world that could be spoiling it?

PSHE
Another meaning of the word *measure* can be *to measure yourself against another person*. This does not always mean to stand beside someone and to measure size. Explain to the children that it can mean to look at someone in admiration, or envy or to wish you were like someone else. The other person might be happier, richer, more successful, cleverer or kinder than you are. Have the children ever felt like this, and could they describe their feelings? Is there anything they can do about it?

Music
Use musical flashcards, as in Figure 10, for this session, either made by yourself or by the children to remind the class of some traditional Western music notation. You could all look in a hymn book or song book to see some of this notation. Explain that this is a

musical language used all over the world and it never changes.

Show them the three time signatures 2, 3 and 4, explaining that the top number means how many beats are in a bar. A bar is a measurement of time in music. The next card to be shown should be a bar line, which divides the notes up into equal portions (twos, threes and fours). Recap on the values of notes (1 beat, 2 beats and so on). You will also need to look at the double bar line which is placed at the end of a piece of music.

Ask the children to build up lines of rhythms with you. Make sure the value in each bar is the same as indicated in the time signature. The children could then make some cards of their own, and in pairs, create rhythms. It would be interesting to see if the children can play their own rhythms on any of the instruments and then play them to the whole class.

Art

Take into the classroom either a picture of, or an example of, the work of Clarice Cliff, that shows her bold and unusual designs. She created some very bizarre designs which were both colourful, angular and often geometric. They give the impression of being carefully measured designs. Talk with the children about them and ask them to think about how they could create similar designs. Suggest that they use these designs on a piece of plain, A4 white paper as wrapping paper. Once the design has been drawn give everyone the opportunity to paint the shapes in bright colours.

D&T

Ask the children to design and make a gift carrier using the paper created in Clarice Cliff style. Give everyone a sheet of A4 paper for the design notes and on it they should consider: what small toy they might put in the bag as a gift, the bag design, what the dimensions of the bag would be, which materials could be used and how it will be assembled. Once all of this information is recorded, the children could use their painted wrapping paper and make the bag.

PE

Warm the children up, preferably outside, by running round the track, hall, field or playground, turning in response to the sound of a whistle. Divide the class into three groups. They will need to take it in turns to measure and to time the activities.

Group 1 will be working on ball-throwing skills, using rounders balls, cricket balls or footballs, either throwing from a standing position, measuring each throw, or from a sitting position. Each throw should be measured so that each person can aim to improve their performance.

Group 2 will be using their jumping skills. Set up apparatus for them to long jump (provide mats, if necessary), hop, skip and jump and high jump. Again encourage accurate measuring.

Group 3 will be running timed 100 metres, with the time being measured on a stopwatch.

The aim of these activities is not the competition, but the measuring of achievement against themselves. Move the groups around so that everyone tries each activity. Ensure that the activities are safely supervised.

NOW OR LATER

■ Look at some different kinds of calendars and diaries to see how the time of year is measured. The dates, months and year will all be the same but they will be presented in a slightly different way. Ask the children to note the similarities and differences. Give the children this well-known rhyme to learn if they do not already know it:

> 30 days have September, April, June and November
> All the rest have 31 except in February alone,
> Which has but 28 days clear
> And 29 in each leap year.

The children could design their own calendars, using this verse. (English/art/D&T)
■ Ask the children to create a barometer for measuring air pressure (in millibars). Cut the top off a balloon and stretch it over a plastic container. Attach a straw or stick to the centre of the balloon, pointing outwards. Place a sheet of paper behind the experiment and mark on it where the stick is pointing. If you have a barometer, take the first reading from this. Each time the air pressure changes the balloon will expand or deflate causing the stick to move either up or down. The new stick position should be marked to show the changes. (science)
■ Using some of the ideas shown in the Kon Tiki raft and Noah's ark activities on pages 44 and 45, ask the children to design a survival boat for themselves. (D&T)

SHAKESPEARE'S LAND

RESOURCES
You will need:
■ a lady's dress, apron, cloak, bonnet and shoes (Tudor style); paper, writing materials (English)
■ fraction and decimal cards, A4 squared paper, paper, writing materials (mathematics)
■ bulbs, bulb holders, batteries, wire, clips, paperclips, clothes pegs wrapped in foil, drawing pins (science)
■ picture of a Tudor house, paper, writing materials (history)
■ brown envelope and letter (see activity), wall map, several road atlases (geography)
■ prayer wheel, paper, writing materials (RE)
■ xylophone, tambour/tambourine, recorder/glockenspiel (music)
■ cardboard, papier mâché, paint, feathers, sequins, wooden sticks (art)
■ a recording of *Greensleeves*, tape recorder (PE).

WHAT TO DO
English
Take the Tudor clothes into the classroom. Ask for a volunteer (boy or girl) to dress. Then pose the question *If this were 1598 what might he/she be doing?* The children will give many options but lead them towards *an actor*. Explain that it was the boys who were the actors and they took all the ladies' parts. Have the children any ideas about the kind of plays they might have been in? (Stories from the Bible, comedies, historical plays.)

Shakespeare's plays always asked for young actors. The actors used to travel from one town to another, performing in large houses, squares, inn yards and other public places. Ask the children to imagine that they are young actors and how they might

OBJECTIVES
■ writing prose and newspaper reports; dramatising and writing playscripts **(English)**
■ working with fractions and decimals; breaking down complex calculations **(mathematics)**
■ wiring a circuit with a switch **(science)**
■ investigating Tudor streets and houses **(history)**
■ locating places then planning a route **(geography)**
■ writing a prayer **(RE)**
■ understanding the value of working together **(PSHE)**
■ creating music for a dance **(music)**
■ using materials to create 3-D artefacts **(art)**
■ creating a dance **(PE)**

47

spend the day. Read the following text to the class, which shows a day in the life of one imaginary child actor.

When dawn rises, I have to read through the script for *Romeo and Juliet* to remember my lines. I have to be out of bed by 8.00 sharp, in order to be at the theatre by 8.15, otherwise I will be fined. At 9.00, when all of the parts have been allocated, we start rehearsing.

At 11.30, I dash out to get hot pies, and order some ale for other members of the cast. At 12.00 sharp, I get to have a look at the new play, *A Midsummer Night's Dream*, ready to perform in the future.

Our first performance of *Romeo and Juliet* is at 2.00, and I am very nervous, as I haven't played this part before. By 2.30, I am on stage, playing the part of a ladies' maid. The play is over by 3.30, and it went down well – the audience clapped very loudly.

At 6.30, I have to load all the costumes and props onto the cart, ready to go to a new venue for an evening performance. It is a very long day, and I finally go to bed at 10.30.

Discuss the kind of life that this child would have had. Ask the children to write their own version using the title 'My day as an actor in 1598'. Listen to some of them.

Have any of the children recently been to the theatre? What did they see? Encourage a wide variety of suggestions, such as pantomimes, puppet shows, variety shows, plays and musicals. Ask them to describe the theatre they have visited. Most theatres have a stage and raised seats but theatres in Shakespeare's time were different. They were open air but the players were sheltered by a roof painted to look like the sky. Most of the audience stood to watch the plays but there were a few seats for the wealthy. There were only two exits. If the audience didn't like the play they would throw cabbages or other rotten vegetables at the players. There was one famous theatre called 'The Globe' which was sadly burnt to the ground during a performance of *Henry VIII*. Ask the children to imagine that they were at this performance, which had attracted a full house, in their role as reporter for a news board. How did they hear about the fire? What happened? Where did they go? What did they see? Ask some of the children to read their reports to the rest of the class.

Read to the children 'The Witches' Brew' (below) from *Macbeth*, Act IV, Scene I.

Fillet of a fenny snake,
In the cauldron boil and bake:
Eye of newt and toe of frog,
Wool of bat and tongue of dog,
Adder's fork and blind-worm's sting,
Lizard's leg and owlet's wing,
For a charm of powerful trouble,
Like a hell-broth boil and bubble.

Double, double toil and trouble:
Fire burn and cauldron bubble.

The witches play an important part in *Macbeth*, in fact they open the play accompanied by thunder and lightening. Invite the children to create a list of other suitable words for a witches' brew based on Shakespeare's and encourage them to write their own in a similar style. Divide the class into small groups for each to read their spell. Ask each group to choose the best and to dramatise the scene of the witches, chanting their spell around the cauldron.

Read to the children the following passing adapted from *Macbeth* (Act I, Scene III), suggesting to them that they will be writing their own play about this scene.

After the battle, Macbeth – Thane of Glamis, and another Scottish general called Banquo were returning home. It was getting dark, lightning was flashing and thunder rolled around. As they walked across the black heath they were astonished to see three creatures who looked like women but were not women. Their strange clothes, withered skin and straggly beards made them look unearthly. They seemed frightened when Macbeth spoke to them because they all put a vile finger upon their skinny lips, suggesting that he should not speak. Then the first creature greeted Macbeth by his title, Thane of Glamis. Macbeth was surprised that they knew his name. The next one called him Thane of Cawdor, which was not his name and he was astonished when the third strange woman called him *King that will be*. These strange women were telling of an impossible future. There was no chance that Macbeth would be King, because the King already had two sons. The strange creatures had a message for Banquo too. He would be lesser than Macbeth but greater, happier than Macbeth, and although he would never be King, his sons would inherit the throne. Macbeth and Banquo watched with amazement as the three strange creatures disappeared into the night. When they had recovered themselves, they stood together discussing what they had seen and heard.

Ask the children: *Where does it take place? Who are the main characters? What time of day is it?* Encourage the children to plan the sequence of events:
1. The witches discussing their spells.
2. Macbeth and Banquo riding home.
3. Macbeth and Banquo meet the witches.
4. They talk to the witches.
5. The witches leave.
6. Macbeth and Banquo discuss what has happened.

Explain that in play writing, normal speech is used and the characters' names are written each time they speak. Give the children a starting point using familiar English, such as:

1st Witch:	What did you put in your latest brew?	
2nd Witch:	Treacle, honey, insects and mice.	
3rd Witch:	Didn't you use…	

Listen to some of the children's playlets, and if there is time, give the children an opportunity to act out some of their scenes in small groups.

Mathematics

Explain to the children that in Shakespeare's time there was no television, so many people went to the theatre. How many of the children have been to the theatre? Is it half, more than half, or less than half of the class? Take a set of fraction and decimal cards into the classroom to use to remind the children of the value of each. At random, turn one over and display it to the children, discuss it and then repeat the exercise. Each child should cut out a set of fraction and decimal cards so that they can respond as you display a number. For example, when you display the '¼' card, they should hold up the '0.25' card.

In pairs, the children can play a memory game with one child holding all the fraction cards and the other child holding all the decimal cards. As each pair finishes, encourage them to play pelmanism where all the cards are placed downwards and the children turn the cards over to make matching decimal and fraction pairs.

Day of week	No. of tickets sold	Amount paid
Monday	18	
Tuesday	16	
Wednesday	12	
Thursday	15	
Friday	19	
Saturday	20	

Figure 11

Refer to Figure 11, which shows ticket sales for a performance of a Shakespeare play at the Royal Shakespeare Theatre in Stratford-upon-Avon. Write these on the flip chart and tell the children that one ticket costs £15.50. Discuss together possible ways of calculating the total amount of money paid for each day's ticket sales. Then give everyone the opportunity to use their own method. Check the results as a whole class.

Figure 12 shows the number of pages included in a programme for a Shakespeare play at the Royal Shakespeare theatre. A different number of pages is allocated for particular information and there are 18 pages altogether. Write the information on the flip chart. The children should then calculate the fraction of the whole programme that each item requires. They should then be able to represent the fractions as a pie chart.

Ask the children to imagine they are to design a poster to advertise the play *Macbeth* on Saturday 30 July at 7.30pm at the Globe Theatre in London. There must be sufficient space for the illustrations. Hand the children the squared paper, and tell them that the advertisers require some information. They need to know where and how much space there will be for the title, date, time, price, illustrations and the name of the theatre. Ask them to mark out each of these areas on their squared paper. When all of these are in place, ask what fraction of the paper is left. This could be calculated by looking at the squares and counting those left

Information to include	No. of pages
Introduction	1
General advertising	11
Names of cast and orchestra	2
Synopsis of the play	1
Information about other performances	3

Figure 12

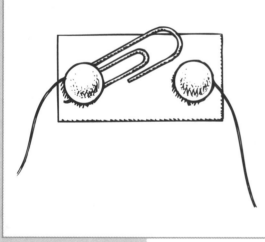

Figure 13

Science
Can the children make a list of the things in their home that use electricity? What do they think would be different about the kind of house that Shakespeare would have lived in? Ask: *What would people use for light and heat? If they had had the knowledge and the resources that we have today how would they have lit their homes?* Can the children remember how to wire a circuit? What do they need? (Bulb, bulb holder, battery, wire and clips.) Ask them to work in pairs to wire a circuit, to reinforce previous experience. How could they use this circuit in a home? They will need to discuss how to switch it on and off.

Ask the pairs to experiment completing and breaking the circuit, using either paper clips, clothes pegs wrapped in foil, drawing pins or anything else they can suggest that conducts electricity (see Figure 13).

Finally, they should draw the circuit, including the switch, using the correct symbols (see Figure 14).

—⊣ ▮—	battery
—⊖—	bulb
——	wire
—⊓—	buzzer
▭—◯—▭	motor
—⦁—	joining two wires
—∘⁄ ∘—	open switch
—∘—∘—	closed switch

Figure 14

History
Set a scene, introducing the children to the idea of a street in Tudor times, by reading the following quotation from *Town Life* by Tony Triggs:

'In every street carts and coaches make such a thundering. Hammers are beating, pots clinking. There are porters sweating under burdens and merchants carrying bags of money.'

Show the children the picture of a Tudor house. Discuss with the children how people lived. *How is this house different from a modern house?* (Wattle and daub, wooden beams, lead pipes, tall chimneys, brick foundations, carpenter's marks and so on.) *Has anyone seen a Tudor house? Where?* Many of the houses in Stratford-upon-Avon where Shakespeare lived are Tudor houses. He would have lived in one of them. The windows are small but if he had looked out of one of these leaded windows, what do the children think he would have seen? (Narrow streets, rows of timbered houses, layered houses with the top floor overhanging the floor beneath it.) Many houses had a jetty which overhangs the floor beneath it. In tall houses there were several of these. Can the children suggest why houses needed these? (The streets were so narrow that it made more space in the higher rooms and so the rubbish thrown out of the windows did not hit anyone – there was no drainage or sanitation.) The streets were very smelly and dirty with open drains. Discuss the differences between now and then.

Divide the class into groups of six and ask five members of each group to take on the role of a character who would be in the street. They should each write down details of what they would be doing. The sixth member of each group should take on the role of a reporter who will interview the other group members and ask them to explain what they are doing.

Geography

You will need a brown official-looking envelope containing a representation of a letter from a newspaper to say that the class have won a competition to go to Stratford-upon-Avon to see *Macbeth* the following Saturday. Where is Stratford-upon-Avon? Do the children know how to get there? Using individual atlases they should be encouraged to find it. Who can find it first? Encourage everyone to locate the place. Relate this to information on a wall map and attach a label to mark the town. The children will need to know where the school is in relation to Stratford-upon-Avon. By looking at the map, which method of transport will they choose to use? They will in fact be going by coach so it would be useful to obtain a route description beforehand from the Internet, AA, or a road map. Decide with the children the main towns, cities and counties that the route would follow and ask them to list them. Using this information and any other they can find from their own atlas, the children should present a sketch map including compass directions to show their routes. Ask the children to write a brief description of the journey.

RE

Tell the children how the Buddists of Tibet carry around prayer wheels. Explain to them that these are beautifully decorated cylindrical objects on a handle so that they can be held, and that inside is a sacred mantra. Ask if any of the children can tell you what a mantra is. Explain that it is like a prayer, but that it doesn't have to be written down or even spoken, it can just be uplifting or spiritual thoughts. Explain that the prayer wheel moves when revolved by hand and that each turning represents the mantra being spoken or thought of.

Tell the children that they are going to write their own mantra and that these are to be written in the style of a sonnet. A sonnet has sixteen lines and rhyming couplets. Ask the children for suggestions as to what they would like their mantra to be about (the weather, family, friends, animals, countryside and so on) and to write eight lines of a prayer in sonnet style, and when they have finished, read the prayers together. For example:

Thank you for this lovely day
This is what I'd like to pray.
Thank you for the warmth and sun
Helping me to get things done.
Thank you for the flowers so bright
And the stars we see at night.
Thank you for our daily food
Keep us healthy, fit and good.

PSHE

What do the children think would be the most satisfying part of being in a play like *Macbeth*? Lead them towards a discussion of the values of working together. *Why is it important?* When do they need to work together in other activities? Divide the class into small groups and delegate one member (without the others knowing) to be controversial. Ask the group to have a discussion on, for example, the school football team, the conservation garden, school pond or something that is of current interest in the school. Invite them to report back on how disruptive the extra controversial contribution was.

Music

Give each small group the selection of the instruments to create music for a Tudor circle dance. The xylophone must only play an ostinato (repeating the same notes) of F (high and low together) in a rhythm. The recorder players/glockenspiels create any tune on the notes F, G, A and Bb in a rhythm to fit above the ostinato. The tambour/tambourine then adds musical decoration to this. Each group should build up their tune by beginning with (a) ostinato then add (b) the tune and then add (c) other instruments. They might like to create a circle dance to this music.

Art

Tell the children they are going to make a lorgnette mask (eye cover with a handle) for one of the witches in *Macbeth*, using papier mâché. They must draw and cut out their shape on the cardboard, then build up the features using the papier maché. Encourage long noses, big eyebrows and wrinkled foreheads. Give the models time to dry and then ask the children to paint, dry and decorate them. Once complete the masks should be attached to the wooden stick to be held across the eyes.

PE

Play or sing *Greensleeves* to the children and invite everyone to create their own slow movements to the music. (For example, forwards, backwards, turn, sideways movements, turn, bow, curtsey.) This can be developed in pairs and eventually in fours. Play the music again and ask the children to imagine they are in the hall of a large Tudor home dancing together.

NOW OR LATER

■ *Life in Shakespeare's England was better than it is today.* Discuss and debate. (English)
■ Open sewers, filth in the streams, flies, holes in the ground for toilets and dirty streets in Tudor times were a health hazard. Ask the children how these have been improved to promote healthy living. (science)
■ As a class, look at some pictures of people in traditional Tudor costume. Discuss with the children the kinds of materials that might have been used to make the clothes (velvet, elaborate buttons, silk, lace, leather, brocade and so on). The children should design their own Tudor costume, making suggestions as to what they would use and how they would use it. (D&T)

SUNNY ISLANDS

RESOURCES

You will need:
■ paper, writing materials, dictionaries, reference books on the Caribbean, bunch of bananas (English)
■ 100 counting sticks or straws of different colours for each group, copies of photocopiable pages 62 and 63 for each child, paper, writing and colouring materials (mathematics)
■ soil, water, plastic bottle, plastic jug, gravel, sand, cotton wool, paper towel and filter paper for each group (science)
■ a potato, flip chart or board, paper, writing materials (history)
■ world map, travel brochures, paper, writing materials (geography)
■ flip chart or board, paper, writing materials (PSHE)
■ xylophones, chime bars and tambourines for each group (music)
■ books with examples of Aubrey Williams's work, pastels, paint, white glue, collage materials, paper (art)
■ paper, writing materials (D&T)
■ sponge balls, skittles, hoops, large balls and rackets (PE).

WHAT TO DO

English

Ask the children to imagine that they have just arrived on a sunny island somewhere in the Caribbean. Divide the class into small groups to discuss their initial reactions to being in this completely different environment and after a short time bring all the ideas together. Encourage them to write a letter home describing their feelings and observations. Collect together some useful words from the discussion, both nouns and adjectives such as *climate*, *beach*, *vegetation*, *shacks*, *hot*, *colourful*, *clean*, *windy* and so on. Give the children an example of a letter format to include an imaginary address, a new island name, a suggested date and greeting.

Ask the children to write an informative report about a Caribbean island, giving details of the climate, the weather and the vegetation. They should look up in the dictionary the meaning of these words and reinforce this by using reference books from the classroom or library to research them. This research could be carried out with a partner before they write a collaborative report. The children should compare the conditions with those at home. Ask some of the pairs to read out their reports.

Take a bunch of bananas into the classroom for the children to look at. Discuss together how they will have been grown on the island, who will have harvested them and how they could be used (soup, bread, sweet, cake, braised as a vegetable). Read a simple recipe (below) to them.

OBJECTIVES

■ writing letters, reports and recipes; writing rhyming acrostic poems; role-playing interviews **(English)**
■ calculating percentages **(mathematics)**
■ devising experiments to demonstrate that materials can be separated by filtering **(science)**
■ dramatising or writing about a significant person in history **(history)**
■ studying a distant location **(geography)**
■ considering how people's beliefs are communicated **(RE)**
■ reflecting on their own feelings and the feelings of others **(PSHE)**
■ appreciating and creating music in the style of other cultures **(music)**
■ exploring different methods (pastels, paints and collages) to communicate observations **(art)**
■ planning, designing and making a sun hat **(D&T)**
■ practising ball control skills **(PE)**

BANANA BREAD
Ingredients
75g margarine
110g caster sugar
One egg
225g self-raising flour
4 peeled bananas
rind and juice of one lemon and one orange

Directions
1. Preheat the oven to gas mark 4 or 180°C.
2. Grease a loaf tin, size 9 x 19cm.
3. Beat together the margarine and the sugar.
4. Beat the egg and then beat it into the margarine and sugar.
5. Mash the bananas and add the lemon and orange rind and juice.
6. Blend with the other ingredients.
7. Spoon the mixture into the loaf tin.
8. Place in the oven for 50 minutes.

Divide the class into pairs for each pair to create a new banana recipe. It can include sugar, milk, ice cream, water, flour and margarine as well as the fruit. The recipe must include the ingredients, method, cooking time and presentation.

Give the children the letters of *DESERT ISLAND* so that they can create an acrostic poem with rhyming couplets. Practise writing rhyming couplets to begin with. For example:

Days seem slow on our island
Everything moves in dreams
Sometimes it's hot and humid
Everything's sleepy it seems
Rainbow colours are vivid
Trousers and tops are short.

I love being on our island
Scenes of every sort
Let's stay on this island
And keep on enjoying the sun
No one to worry us, no one to hurry us
Days are full of fun.

The children may have heard of the BBC radio programme *Desert Island Discs* where a person is asked to choose pieces of music, a book and a special thing to take with them if they are marooned on a desert island. Invite everyone to write down two pieces of music, a book and one special thing they would hope to have with them on their island. Make sure the children understand that they need to choose durable goods of lasting value. Set up a scene for one child to interview another with the interviewer asking questions about the choices. Invite constructive comments.

Mathematics

Tell the children to imagine a very hot day on a sunny island. They are to be ice-cream sellers and need to check how many lollies they have for sale. Use coloured counting sticks, straws or cubes to represent the lollies. Give each group of children 100 counting sticks, straws or cubes of different colours. Ask them to count how many there are of each colour. For example, 12 green sticks, 26 red sticks, 14 yellow sticks, 20 blue sticks and 28 orange sticks. *What is the percentage of each?* Tell the children that *percent* means of a hundred, therefore 26 = 26%. Do they recognise

the % sign? Ask the children to work through photocopiable page 62 where they will colour squares to represent a specific percentage of a given number.

Carry out the following example with the children. 20 children have red sunglasses, 35 have brown ones and 45 are wearing blue ones. *What percentage have red sunglasses?* Refer the children back to photocopiable page 62 so that they can work through some examples for themselves.

Ask the children to imagine that they are visiting a holiday discount shop on a sunny island. What kind of things do they think might be for sale? They might suggest sunglasses, suntan lotion, bikinis, swimming trunks, insect repellent, sandals and so on. Tell them that everything is reduced in price by 10%. Show the children how to divide the original price (for example, £5.60) by 10 to give the discount (in this case, of 56p). They should take the discount away from the original price to give the discounted price (£5.04). Now tell them that a lilo costs £12. *If the discount is 10%, what is the sale price?* (£11.80) Give the children the following sale items to practise their percentages:

- sunglasses £5
- suntan lotion £4
- insect repellent £3
- bikini £15
- trunks £8
- sunhat £6
- sandals £12
- beach bag £9
- floating duck £14

Ask the children to suggest what kind of food they would expect to see on a restaurant menu on a sunny island (for example, tropical fruit salad, Caribbean chicken, avocado salad, barbecued fish, banana milk shake, mango squash). Discuss the information given on photocopiable page 63. Again remind the children of the procedure for calculating percentages. Ask the children to work through the activities.

Make a list of the fruits for sale in a local supermarket which would also be readily available on a sunny island. These might include kiwi fruit, mangoes, papaya, bananas, star fruits, coconuts and guavas. Suggest a realistic price for a piece of fruit on sale locally and tell them that on the island the fruit is 15% cheaper. Ask the children to suggest how they could find out the island price. Give some examples to show how to calculate 10%, then 5%, and then to add the two together to give 15%. Explain that they must then deduct this amount from the original price to find the reduced price. Ask the children to reduce the following items by 15%:

- guavas 60p
- melon £1.65
- mango 95p
- papaya £1.05
- banana 15p
- star fruit 30p
- pineapple £1.25

Science

Take into the classroom some soil and water to show the children and ask them to make a link with desert islands. Direct the children towards the fact that much of the water on a desert island would be muddy and contain bacteria and other impurities. Ask the children: *Why do we need clean water?* (To drink, wash, do the washing and prepare food.) Pour the water into the soil to create mud and explain that this happens when it rains.

Divide the children into small groups, each group with a plastic bottle with the top cut off to make a filter, and a selection of gravel, sand, soil, cotton wool, paper towels or filter papers and water. There are two stages to the experiment, first to make the water dirty and then to make it clean again. Ask them to plan what they will do and to make a prediction or hypothesis for the result and then to carry out the investigation (see Figure 15). Encourage them to discuss, evaluate and record their results. Some groups could present their findings to the whole class.

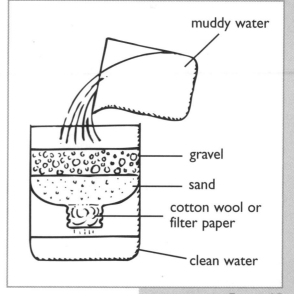

muddy water

gravel

sand

cotton wool or filter paper

clean water

Figure 15

History

Show the children a potato. Do they know how the potato first came to Ireland and then to England? A famous explorer went to America and brought some back with him. He was called Sir Walter Raleigh and he lived between 1552–1618. Can the children say what an explorer is? Would they like to be explorers? Would they feel like explorers on their sunny island? Why? Read the story of Sir Walter Raleigh (see next page) to the class, and talk about some of the important details.

The story of Sir Walter Raleigh could be dramatised by the children using the headings, 'Preparing to board the ship', 'Life at sea' or 'Exploring the island'. Alternatively they could assume the role of Sir Walter Raleigh and write of their experiences.

Sir Walter Raleigh (1552–1618)

Sir Walter Raleigh was born at Budleigh Salterton in Devon around 1552. He studied at Oxford University but left to fight against the Catholics. Later he went to Ireland to suppress the rebellion there.

Sir Walter Raleigh helped to finance the first English voyage of exploration across the Atlantic Ocean to North America in 1584. He also sent a second expedition in 1585, headed by his cousin Sir Richard Grenville who began a settlement on Roanoke Island. Sir Walter Raleigh himself went on a third expedition to the area and named the land 'Virginia'. He was one of the first Europeans to smoke tobacco which was brought back by the second expedition. He also introduced potatoes to Ireland.

He was a favourite of Queen Elizabeth I. At court he entertained her with stories of his adventures. In 1588 he organised the defence of Devon against the Spanish Armada. However he fell out of favour with her when he married one of her maids of honour in 1592.

Anxious to discover gold which he had been told was in South America, he set sail in 1595. He only managed to find quartz, a rock with specks of gold in it.

Unfortunately, when Elizabeth died, the new king, James I, did not like him. He was accused of treason and was sentenced to life imprisonment in the Tower of London. Whilst he was there he wrote a book called *History of the World*. He was released in 1616 and persuaded the king to allow him to search again for gold in South America. He failed to find any and on his return in 1618 James I ordered his execution.

Geography

Ask the children if they know where the Caribbean Sea is. Show them a world map and ask a volunteer to locate it. Look at it in relation to the UK. Find the equator and relate both places to it. What do they think would be the main differences between living in the Caribbean and living in the UK? (Hours of sunshine, rainfall and so on.)

Have some travel brochures to show the children with details of hours of sunshine and rainfall for different places. Encourage them to make comparisons together. Ask the children to make lists showing how the sunshine and rainfall will create a different way of living. (For example, outdoor activities, indoor activities, different foods, clothes and drinks and so on.)

RE

Do the children know what a missionary is? (A person who gives up everything to tell other people about their faith.) A missionary does not have to go abroad to do this but most people assume that they do. In the 19th century many missionaries travelled to what were considered exotic and remote places abroad. Tell the children the story of David Livingstone below.

David Livingstone

David Livingstone was a Scottish doctor and missionary. He was born in Blantyre and at the age of ten started work in a cotton mill. He was determined to be educated and to become a doctor. He studied at night school and even took his books to the mill. At the age of 25 he was accepted by the London Missionary Society to train as a doctor, and in 1840 he qualified. Livingstone wanted to go to China, but was sent to Africa. On arrival he set about learning the local language and to study the ways of the people. This made his task of spreading God's word and treating the people's ailments much easier. He believed that God had called him to help the people of Africa, to open up the continent to European ideas and trade, and by so doing, destroy the evils he saw around him – slavery, poverty and disease.

Livingstone travelled extensively in Africa, preaching and healing, and as time passed he became a famous explorer. He did not forget that he was a missionary, but exploring became almost as important.

Perhaps the most famous story relating to Doctor Livingstone is his meeting with Stanley, an American journalist, at Ujiji. Livingstone had disappeared for over five years and most people had given him up for dead. Stanley set out to find him and did so, greeting him with the now immortal words, 'Doctor Livingstone, I presume.' Stanley wanted Livingstone to return with him to London, but Livingstone refused. He was determined to continue with the work he was convinced that God had called him to do, preaching, healing and exploring. All the travel had taken its toll of Livingstone's health. He had been ill many times. On 1 May 1873 his faithful African companions found him dead, kneeling beside his bed where he had been praying. They embalmed his body and carried it 1500 miles to the coast from where it was taken back to Britain. Livingstone, a brave and tender-hearted man, was buried in Westminster Abbey.

PSHE

Introduce the idea of solitude by reading the poem below.

Alone
In a world I have made
Surrounded by the things I love
Content, knowing that all is well.
No one to speak to
No need to listen
My own space
Solitude.

Is this how they feel when they are alone? Where would they go to be alone? How would they feel on an desert island? Maybe some children are never alone and would like to be. Ask them: *Why is it good to be alone sometimes?* Collect words for your flip chart to inspire the children to write about solitude (stress the point that solitude is not loneliness) and invite them to create their own poems.

Music

One of the most popular Caribbean songs is called a calypso. The song *Linstead Market* ('Tar ra Boom de ay') is a good example of a Jamaican calypso. A calypso is in time with a jumping rhythm and tells of events happening on the island. In small groups, invite the children to perform this calypso remembering that calypsos have a lot of repetition and are often humorous.

Yesterday with Mary May
I went to buy some clothes
Yesterday with Mary May
I went to buy some clothes
Some were bright and some had laces
Some had holes in unfortunate places
Some were pretty and others sad
Some would have suited my Grandad
Yesterday with Mary May
I went to buy some clothes.

Ask the children to play the notes of F, G, A, B flat, C, D, E and F on the tuned percussion instruments (xylophone, chime bars). Every person in the group could create a tune for two of the lines, using these notes, and then they could be put together. Encourage others to accompany the tune with tambourines playing throughout. The children may be able to create a calypso of their own. It could be about a shopping expedition to the holiday discount shop in the earlier maths activity on page 54.

Art

If it is possible, show the children some of the work of Aubrey Williams in which he portrays the colour of Caribbean life. Focus on the bird pictures in which he takes the general shape of a bird and creates an exotic, colourful representation. If this is not possible, use any other pictures of Caribbean birds that you can find in encyclopedias or on the Internet. Encourage the children to copy the pictures of the birds and then to elaborate with colourful designs, either in pastels, paint mixed with white glue or collage. These could be the birds that the children could see on their sunny island.

D&T

On a sunny island the children will need to protect their heads from the midday sun. Ask them to plan and design a sun hat to exact measurements. They will need to decide on the design criteria (lightweight, close weave, firm, strong) and what materials they could use to make it. With a partner the children should measure the circumference of the other person's head and cut a strip of paper to correspond. They will need to consider which parts of the head need most protection (top of the head, eyes, back of the neck). Ask them to design a sun hat to fulfil these requirements and cut out a paper pattern.

PE

Tell the children that football and cricket are popular sports in the Caribbean. The children may be able to talk about some famous teams. Give everyone a small sponge ball, to use in a variety of ways in a controlled situation (dribbling, bouncing, catching, patting). Ask some children to demonstrate their skills. Repeat the activity to show improvement. Working in pairs, ask them to practise throwing and catching.

Make a slalom using skittles and hoops for all the children to show control of a ball around it. Divide the class into four groups and set up activities in four areas to develop throwing (for example, netball), dribbling (football), aiming (cricket) and hand control (using tennis racquets). The children should move from one activity to the next so that everyone has a turn at each skill.

NOW OR LATER

■ Ask the children to suggest materials that could be used to build a temporary living space on the island. Then tell them to classify them under the headings, 'changed by heat' / 'not changed by heat'. (science)

■ Ask the children to use reference books to find out about the different animals which live in a hot sunny climate. What differences are there between these and those living in a cold climate? (geography)

■ Ask the children to make a collection of materials that might be found on a sunny island (sand, pebbles, wood, string, straws, leaves and so on). Encourage them to use these to build up a natural collage of an island. (art)

■ Make the banana bread as shown in the recipe. How do the children think it could be improved? (D&T)

Colour in the garden

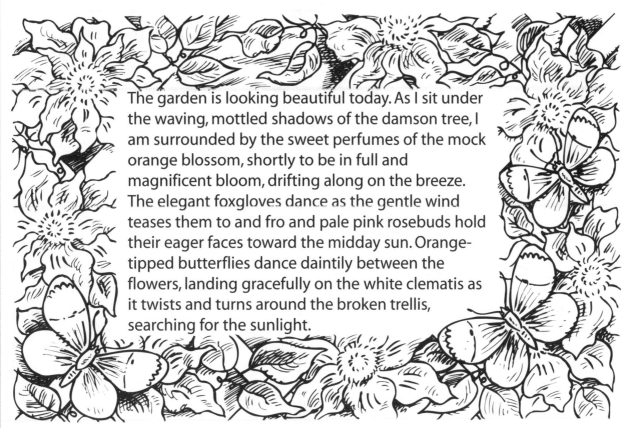

The garden is looking beautiful today. As I sit under the waving, mottled shadows of the damson tree, I am surrounded by the sweet perfumes of the mock orange blossom, shortly to be in full and magnificent bloom, drifting along on the breeze. The elegant foxgloves dance as the gentle wind teases them to and fro and pale pink rosebuds hold their eager faces toward the midday sun. Orange-tipped butterflies dance daintily between the flowers, landing gracefully on the white clematis as it twists and turns around the broken trellis, searching for the sunlight.

■ How many adjectives can you find in this passage? Write them in the space below.

■ Use five of your adjectives in sentences of your own.

'What you eat' survey

Look at the pie chart. What does it tell you? Which is most popular? Which is least popular? Place the food in order of demand and write a statement about the chart in the box.

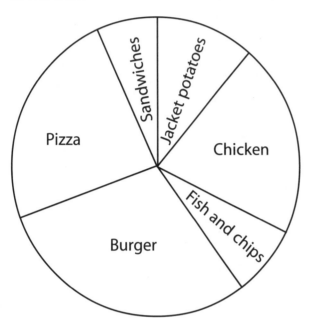

Use your tally chart to show who likes which food in the class. Draw an approximate pie chart and write a statement about it.

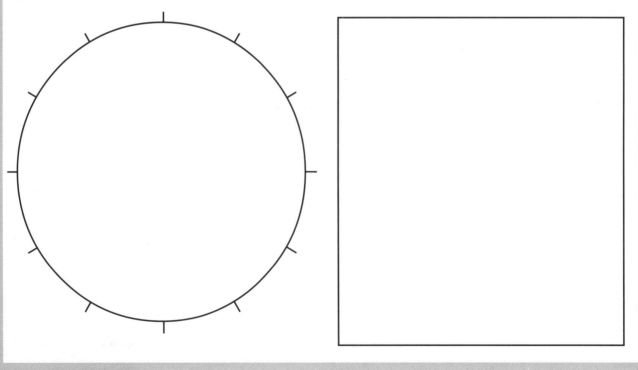

Name   Date

Kon-Tiki

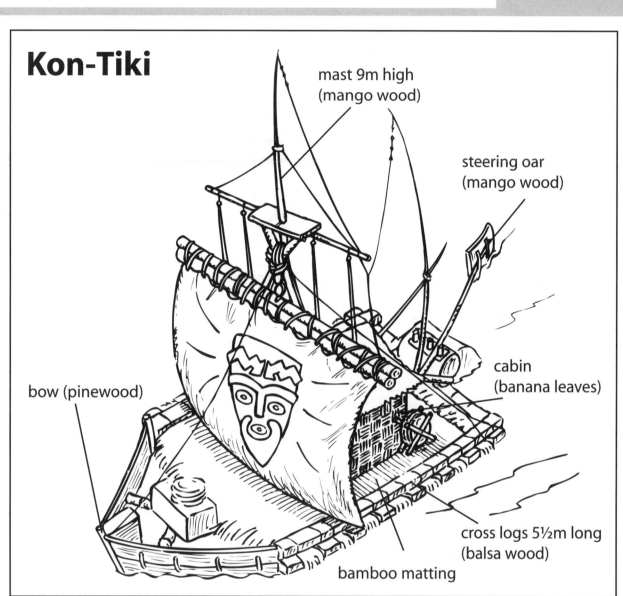

mast 9m high
(mango wood)

steering oar
(mango wood)

bow (pinewood)

cabin
(banana leaves)

cross logs 5½m long
(balsa wood)

bamboo matting

Building Kon-Tiki	Living on Kon-Tiki

What percentage?

■ Colour the given amount.

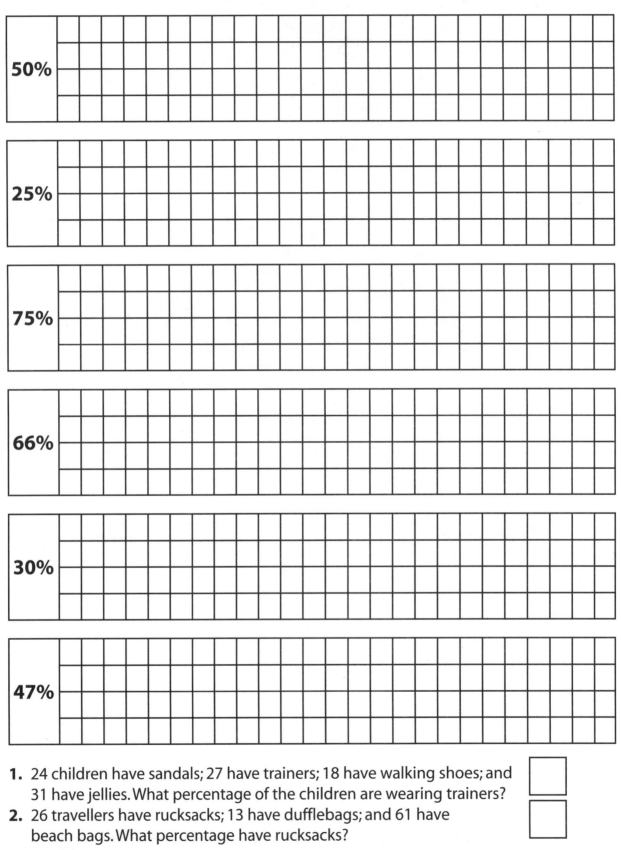

50%

25%

75%

66%

30%

47%

1. 24 children have sandals; 27 have trainers; 18 have walking shoes; and 31 have jellies. What percentage of the children are wearing trainers?

2. 26 travellers have rucksacks; 13 have dufflebags; and 61 have beach bags. What percentage have rucksacks?

What do they eat?

The following till record shows what 60 people at Old Joe's Restaurant chose to eat:

Old Joe's Restaurant

Tropical fruit salad	6
Caribbean chicken	12
Avocado salad	18
Lobster appetiser	5
Salmon and melon cocktail	6
Barbecued fish	4
Mango squash	9

The manager wishes to change the menu, but hopes to retain the most popular choices. What percentage of the people eating chose the following?

Tropical fruit salad ☐   Caribbean chicken ☐   Avocado salad ☐

Salmon and melon cocktail ☐   Mango squash ☐

What percentage of the customers together chose to eat lobster appetiser and barbecued fish? ☐

Skills Index
NATIONAL STANDARDS FOR KEY SKILLS

Ready to go! SUPPLY TEACHING